PRE-INTERMEDIATE

Workbook

T0350684

Link Up

Series Editors

Angela Cussons

Francesca Stafford

Australia • Brazil • Japan • Korea • Mexico • Singapore • Spain • United Kingdom • United States

Link Up Pre-Intermediate Workbook

Series Editors
Angela Cussons
Francesca Stafford

Director of Content Development: Sarah Bideleux

Development Editor: Francesca Stafford

Associate Development Editor: Phillip McElmuray

Art Director: Natasa Arsenidou

Text/cover designer: Tania Diakaki

Cover image: Shutterstock.com

Compositor: Tania Diakaki

Acknowledgements

Contributing writers: Rachel Finnie, Jason Kirby

The publishers would like to thank Visual Hellas for permission to reproduce copyright photographs.

For product information and technology assistance,
contact **emea.info@cengage.com**.

For permission to use material from this text or product, and for permission queries, email **emea.permissions@cengage.com**

British Library Cataloguing-in-Publication Data
A catalogue record for this book is available from the British Library.

ISBN: 978-960-403-641-7

Cengage Learning EMEA
Cheriton House, North Way, Andover, Hampshire, SP10 5BE
United Kingdom

Cengage Learning products are represented in Canada by Nelson Education Ltd.

For your lifelong learning solutions, visit **www.cengage.co.uk**

Purchase your next print book, e-book or e-chapter at **www.cengagebrain.com**

Printed in the United Kingdom by Lightning Source
Print Number: 08   Print Year: 2015

Contents

Unit

Unit 1　Friends and Family

Vocabulary Link

A　Complete the e-mail with these words.

| boring | course | early | exciting | first | Halls of Residence | late | lecturers |

E-mail

New　Reply　Forward　Print　Delete　Send & Receive

Hi Ellen,

Here it is! Your **(1)** _____ e-mail from your little sister!

So, how's university? Are you enjoying the **(2)** _____ , or is it **(3)** _____?
Are the **(4)** _____ at university different from the teachers at school? And what
are the **(5)** _____ like? Do you like the other people who are staying there?

Mum and Dad send lots of love. Mum doesn't believe that you're really getting up so
(6) _____ every day without her there to shout at you! Dad says he hopes you're
studying hard and not staying up too **(7)** _____ every night! I haven't got anything
(8) _____ to tell you, I'm sorry to say. Life here is the same as usual.

I'm looking forward to seeing you when you come home next weekend.

Lots of love,

Mel

B　Circle the correct words.

1　Jason isn't very popular / unkind at school; he hasn't got any friends at all!

2　My parents disagree / disapprove of my new friends because they ride motorbikes.

3　Sheena doesn't see her cousin often because they aren't unfriendly / close .

4　My mum gets angry if I'm impatient / impolite to my grandparents.

5　Weekends in our house are very basic / hectic because there's so much to do.

6　Dan and his brother want to buy a new computer TV / monitor .

7　I think it's very important to be honest / unhelpful with your friends.

8　Dad says students spend too much time in the Students' Hall / Union and not enough time studying.

C Use the words in capitals at the end of each sentence to make words which fit in the spaces.

1 Paula gets extra money every week because she's so _____ in the house.   *HELP*

2 How often do you spend a _____ evening at home with your family?   *RELAX*

3 Having a dog is _____ because there's nobody at home all day.   *PRACTICAL*

4 I hope the other students on the course are _____ .   *FRIEND*

5 Every time Ron brings a new CD home, it _____ ; his brother takes it to his room and we never see it again!   *APPEAR*

6 Leo's crying again! Have you been _____ to him?   *KIND*

7 My family is very noisy and it's _____ to have a quiet chat on the phone!   *POSSIBLE*

8 I love my best friend, but I wish she wasn't so _____ .   *PATIENT*

Grammar Link

D Complete the paragraph with the correct form of the verbs in brackets. Use the Present Simple or the Present Continuous.

Home Sweet Home

My mother **(1)** _____ (shout) at my little brother at the moment. She **(2)** _____ (tell) him that he must do his homework. But she **(3)** _____ (not know) that the TV programme he **(4)** _____ (watch) every week is on right now. My dad and I think that they **(5)** _____ (make) too much noise, so we **(6)** _____ (get) ready to go for a walk in the park. We **(7)** _____ (know) it **(8)** _____ (be) quiet there.

E Match the beginnings of the sentences to their endings.

Beginnings		Endings	
1	Is your grandmother	a	cleans his brand new car.
2	Do your children	b	are getting ready for our cousin's party.
3	Her best friend, Sarah, never	c	watching soap operas again?
4	My brothers and I	d	is cleaning her house today.
5	My son James doesn't	e	watch too much television?
6	My Auntie Jean	f	are painting their house.
7	Every Sunday morning, my father	g	studies for examinations.
8	The next-door neighbours	h	like visiting his cousins.

F Circle the correct words.

1 'Dad, I can smell something; I think the food burns / is burning .'

2 We don't watch / aren't watching quiz shows on TV in our house.

3 Sally's best friend plays / is playing the violin very well; she started learning when she was five!

4 Jim's little sister has / is having a party; that's why he is at my house.

5 Michael's grandfather cooks / is cooking for the whole family every weekend.

6 Do your sisters study / Are your sisters studying at university at the moment?

7 My husband walks / is walking our children to school every morning.

8 'Come and sit at the table,' Mum said, 'the food gets / is getting cold!'

G In each line of this letter there is a word that is not needed. Circle the extra word.

Dear John,

1 *I am writing this letter to be tell you all my family's latest news. Paul*

2 *is complaining that the lessons at his new school are being very difficult.*

3 *Sarah's is learning how to play the trumpet. She practises every day*

4 *for two hours; she is makes too much noise and we are all going*

5 *crazy! Mum and Dad are work hard every day, as usual. Thankfully, their shop*

6 *is never staying open on Sundays, so at least they have one day when*

7 *they can rest. I am fine; I'm not studying a lot these days*

8 *because I want to be getting ready for my exams. I have a lot to learn.*

9 *I hope that you're are well too and that everything is OK.*

10 *I'm looking forward to be hearing from you soon.*

Take care,

Chris

Unit 2 — Legends and Heroes

Vocabulary Link

A Circle the correct words.

What a Hero!

One cold winter's day, while Dave and his best friend Bruce were walking in a **(1)** free / dangerous part of the mountains, Dave fell. Bruce knew that his friend was badly **(2)** injured / favourite and that he had to do something fast.

He was **(3)** determined / fearless to save his friend, so he **(4)** got away / set about finding the quickest way down the mountain. While he was running as fast as his **(5)** big muscles / strong legs would carry him, Bruce said to himself, 'Don't **(6)** give up / grow up , Dave, I'll find someone to rescue you.'

Finally, Bruce found some people and he tried to tell them about his friend. They **(7)** proved / refused to follow him at first, but he **(8)** solved / managed to make them understand that he needed their help, and they all went up the mountain.

Thanks to **(9)** brave / well-built Bruce , the people **(10)** gathered / rescued Dave, and after a few days in hospital he was fine again and ready for another walk in the mountains with his friend. But Dave knows that he's got a lot to thank Bruce for. Bruce is his hero, and he's a very special hero. You see, Bruce is a dog!

B Complete the table. All the words you need are in Unit 2.

	Noun	Adjective	Adverb
1	danger		
2		free	freely
3			courageously
4	truth	true	
5	sadness		
6	bravery		bravely

C Complete the sentences with these words.

action
bow
find out
give up
historian
leading
national
villain

1 According to legend, Robin Hood was a hero, not a _____ .

2 He was the _____ actor in the film *Camelot*; he played King Arthur.

3 How can we _____ more about the story of Alexander the Great?

4 I used to enjoy _____ films when I was younger.

5 Don't ever _____ fighting for the things you believe in.

6 It isn't surprising that William Wallace became a _____ hero.

7 We listened to the _____ talk about his research on Stonehenge.

8 What is more dangerous, a sword or a _____ and arrow?

D Complete the puzzle.

1 Arthur became king when he pulled a _____ out of a stone.

2 The English started to _____ Scotland in 1304.

3 Batman's black _____ makes him look like a bird.

4 Five thousand English soldiers died in the _____ of Stirling Bridge.

5 Robin Hood used to use a bow and _____ when he fought the Sheriff of Nottingham.

6 King Arthur's nephew stole his _____ while Arthur was fighting the war against Lancelot.

7 William Wallace's _____ fought the English many times.

8 After killing a _____ , Saint George became a hero.

Now complete the sentence with the word in the coloured squares.

Many young people think _____ is the greatest hero ever!

Grammar Link

E Complete the sentences with the correct form of the verbs in brackets. Use the Past Simple, the Past Continuous or used to. More than one answer may be possible.

1 Superman _____ (fly) over the buildings to save the falling aeroplane.

2 Robin Hood _____ (steal) from the rich to give to the poor.

3 The Vikings believed that the god called Thor _____ (bang) the clouds with his hammer to make thunder.

4 Alfred the Great _____ (burn) the cakes because he _____ (think) about the war with the Danes.

5 Millions of adults around the world _____ (read) comics when they were children.

6 The boys _____ (not hear) me come in because they _____ (watch) Batman on DVD.

7 My grandfather _____ (tell) us that a monster would come and get us if we didn't behave ourselves.

8 Sam _____ (read) his *Spiderman* comic when he saw a spider climbing up the wall.

F Circle the correct words.

Whose Stories?

When I was a child, my father **(1)** used to tell / was telling me a bedtime story every night before I **(2)** went / was going to sleep. The stories were always about good people who **(3)** was fighting / fought bad people. I don't think they were ever true stories; he **(4)** was making / used to make them up most of the time.

I **(5)** loved / was loving his stories, so I **(6)** didn't mind / wasn't minding when my parents told me that it was time to go to bed. I **(7)** was thinking / used to think that my father was very clever.

Last week, while I **(8)** told / was telling one of those stories to my own son, he told me that I was very clever. I thanked him and then **(9)** continued / was continuing telling the story. When I told my father what had happened, he asked me if I had told my son the truth: that they weren't my stories. 'Of course not,' I answered, 'I want him to think he has the cleverest dad in the world.' My father looked me in the eyes and **(10)** was smiling / smiled . Can you guess what he told me?

G Write a sentence for each of the situations. Use the Past Simple, the Past Continuous or used to. More than one answer is possible.

1   Cleopatra / come from / ancient Egypt

_____

_____

_____

2   when / we / be / young / we / buy / comics every Saturday

_____

_____

_____

3   Spiderman / climb / a building / when / it / start / to rain

_____

_____

_____

4   Wonder Woman / stop / bullets / from the villain's gun

_____

_____

_____

5   in ancient Rome / gladiators / fight / lions

_____

_____

_____

6   King Arthur / rule / the kingdom for many years

_____

_____

_____

Unit 3 — Arts and Crafts

Vocabulary Link

A Complete the text with these words.

| canvases | gifted | original | sculptures | sketch | talent | traditional | works |

For Art Lovers Everywhere

Are you interested in art? Have you ever wanted to find out if you've got hidden artistic
(1) _____? If so, the new Rainbow Art Gallery and Workshop is the place for you.

The owners of Rainbow have gathered together an incredible collection of both **(2)** _____
and modern **(3)** _____ of art. All the items at Rainbow are **(4)** _____
creations, so visitors to the gallery can admire the work of many truly **(5)** _____ artists.
As well as paintings and drawings, you'll find some fantastic **(6)** _____ and pieces
of pottery.

For those of you more interested in creating art rather than looking at it, there are two workshops
which give you the opportunity to see what you can do. With all the paints, brushes, easels,
(7) _____ and **(8)** _____ pads you need, what are you waiting for?

B Complete the words.

1   This is a place where artists work.   s _ _ _ _ _
2   This is a person's ability to remember things.   m _ _ _ _ _
3   An artist can put his canvas on this while he/she paints.   e _ _ _ _
4   This is another word for very big.   h _ _ _
5   We use this to draw things.   p _ _ _ _ _
6   An artist uses this to paint a picture.   p _ _ _ _ _ _ _ _
7   This is a person who takes photographs.   p _ _ _ _ _ _ _ _ _ _ _
8   This is another word for amazing.   i _ _ _ _ _ _ _ _ _

C Circle the correct words.

1 Sabrina made a lovely vase in her painting / pottery class.

2 I wish we had lessons in arts and crafts / drawings at our school.

3 Wow! That's a great piece of sewing; I didn't know you were so decorative / creative !

4 I can do drawings / art of buildings, but not of people!

5 Do you have to pay to go and look at the paintings in art galleries / competitions ?

6 I hope the artist decorating / judging the competition likes my painting!

7 Derek doesn't usually like modern art, but this sculpture really impressed / managed him.

8 John's studying art history at night lessons / school this year.

Grammar Link

D Complete the sentences with the correct form of the verbs in brackets. Use the Past Simple or the Present Perfect Simple.

1 He _____ (make) a sculpture from old bottles. Isn't it beautiful?

2 The artist _____ (paint) his first portrait when he was seven years old.

3 The gallery _____ (not collect) enough paintings for a new exhibition.

4 _____ the students _____ (buy) paintbrushes at the art fair last week?

5 'I _____ (see) many sculptures, but this is one of the best!' said the art teacher.

6 My grandfather _____ (draw) that picture fifty years ago.

7 She _____ (design) twenty dresses for next month's fashion show.

8 _____ he _____ (visit) many galleries?

E In each line of this paragraph there is a word that is not needed. Circle the extra word.

1 Michael Johnson has always was loved making things with his hands. When he was five years old,

2 he has made presents for his friends using anything he could find. He was very creative and

3 talented. When he did became fifteen years old, he told his parents that he wanted to become

4 a great sculptor. After he has finished school, he went to art college where he quickly

5 was became the student that everybody knew. There wasn't a single person in the whole

6 college who didn't have know his name. When he was twenty-one years old, he had his first

7 full exhibition, which all the art magazines had wrote about. Now, at the age of thirty-five,

8 he has had his own studio and gallery and he has made millions of pounds selling his sculptures to the rich and famous.

F Decide which phrase, a or b, completes the second sentence in each pair, so that both sentences have a similar meaning.

1 His painting is not ready yet.
   He _____ the painting yet.
   a has not finished   **b** finished

2 These ancient Greek pots are 2,500 years old.
   The Greeks _____ these pots 2,500 years ago.
   a have made   **b** made

3 John started working in this gallery ten years ago.
   John _____ in this gallery for ten years.
   a worked   **b** has worked

4 Pottery is becoming more and more popular.
   Pottery _____ more popular.
   a became   **b** has become

5 The Chinese were the first to make kites.
   Kite-making _____ in China.
   a began   **b** has begun

6 'Quick! The sewing class started ten minutes ago!'
   'Quick! We _____ the first ten minutes of the sewing class!'
   a missed   **b** have missed

7 'I really want to visit the Louvre.'
   'I _____ the Louvre yet.'
   a did not visit   **b** haven't visited

8 Sarah earned money by making candles when she was at university.
   Sarah _____ candles to earn money when she was at university.
   a made   **b** has made

G Match the beginnings of the sentences to their endings.

Beginnings	Endings
1 Yesterday, the potter	**a** created a sculpture with bottle tops.
2 Because she needed a warm coat,	**b** painted one more self-portrait.
3 The student has never	**c** her grandmother has made one for her.
4 Before he died, the artist	**d** it has been cancelled.
5 She doesn't need to buy a wedding dress;	**e** and it will be exhibited next week.
6 The art students have finished their work	**f** with wood he found lying around.
7 He made all the model cars	**g** her grandmother made one for her.
8 He can't do the metalwork course;	**h** made a beautiful vase.

Vocabulary Link

A Complete the text with these words.

> coastline   emergencies   equipment   first aid   life jacket
> lifeguards   procedures   protect   warn   water

Safety at Sea

The sea can be a dangerous place. But many people who enjoy **(1)** _____ sports on holiday don't know what to do in **(2)** _____ , either on the beach or out at sea. Some people are stupid enough to go out in a speed boat or on a jet ski without a **(3)** _____ . And there are thousands who haven't learned the basics of **(4)** _____ , which is why **(5)** _____ and coastguards are so important!

They can **(6)** _____ you of the risks and **(7)** _____ you from the dangers that are hiding along every **(8)** _____ and on every beach. They have special life-saving **(9)** _____ and they know the emergency **(10)** _____ to use if swimmers are in danger.

B Circle the correct words.

1 The authorities in our area have been assessing / promoting the beaches to make sure they are safe.

2 Have you heard about the new *Tidy the Beach* campaign the local schools have awarded / launched ?

3 I'm glad people are showing an interest / example in protecting sea creatures.

4 The local projects / authorities should warn residents about the dangers of polluting the beaches.

5 Has the water been trained / tested to make sure it's safe to drink?

6 Let's get fish and chips from the souvenir shop / café and eat them on the beach!

7 I love going to the beach when it's deserted / crowded and I'm the only person there.

8 How can we stop tourists suffering / ruining our beautiful coastline?

C Use the words in capitals at the end of each sentence to make words which fit in the spaces.

1 For your own _____ , please do as the lifeguard tells you!   *SAFE*

2 Are you sure this is _____ water?   *DRINK*

3 This beach would be better if there were more sun _____ .   *LOUNGE*

4 The Blue Flag shows _____ that the sea is clean and safe.   *SWIM*

5 The hotel's in a fantastic _____ , but sadly the sea there isn't very clean.   *LOCATE*

6 All the local _____ have been helping to clean the beach this week.   *RESIDE*

7 Dan hurt his foot when he was running along a _____ beach.   *PEBBLE*

8 Lifeguards are trained to be ready for _____ emergencies at any time.   *EXPECT*

D Complete the sentences with the correct prepositions.

1 First prize was awarded _____ the local coastguard.

2 Tara's not interested _____ studying marine biology.

3 Some of the sea creatures in this area are in danger _____ extinction.

4 Have the authorities here applied _____ the FEE for a Blue Flag?

5 They were warned _____ the dangers, but they still spent all day sunbathing.

6 The *Save the Sea Creatures* campaign was launched _____ the local authorities.

7 You must take a beach umbrella to protect you _____ the sun.

8 Is there any access _____ that beach from the cliff?

Grammar Link

E Circle the correct words.

I'm Going on Holiday!

I haven't (1) slept / been sleeping well for about a week now. I am so excited! I am going on holiday tomorrow with my friend Sarah and her family. I have never (2) been / been going abroad before; I can't wait! I have (3) been looking / looked forward to this day for the last six months. I can't believe it has finally (4) arrived / been arriving . Sarah and her family have (5) gone / been going to Spain every summer for the past five years. I have already (6) bought / been buying everything I need: suntan lotion, sun hats and lots of other things too. I have (7) packed / been packing my suitcase for the past two weeks. Mum thinks I have (8) gone / been going mad! Oh, good, it's seven o'clock; time to get up!

F Complete the sentences with the correct form of the verbs in brackets. Use the Present Perfect Simple or the Present Perfect Continuous.

1 _____ they _____ (see) the Lighthouse Museum yet?

2 John _____ (not swim) all day – he just got in the water a few minutes ago.

3 So far, I _____ (visit) ten beaches on this island.

4 The FEE _____ (not award) this beach a Blue Flag.

5 _____ Robert _____ (work) as a lifeguard since 2008.

6 We _____ (try) to reduce the levels of pollution for the last ten years.

7 I _____ (stop) looking for a quiet beach – there aren't any!

8 People _____ (pollute) the sea for too long; it's time they stopped.

G Write a sentence for each of the situations. Use the Present Perfect Simple or the Present Perfect Continuous.

1 the oil tanker / pollute / the sea

_____

_____

4 Sheila / sunbathe / since this morning

_____

_____

2 the fisherman / lose / his boat

_____

_____

5 Maria / learn / to water-ski / for two weeks

_____

_____

3 they / clean up / the beach / for three hours

_____

_____

6 he / swim / to the island

_____

_____

Reading Link

A Read the article quickly and find out who Jim West is.

Holidays that Harm the Sea

Holidaymakers who want a relaxing but exciting break have, for years, been choosing cruises. Cruise ships, which are rather like huge, floating luxury hotels, have got all the facilities you need and give you the chance to admire the coastlines of the world.

Sadly, however, our seas are suffering as cruises are becoming more and more popular, and more pollution is being created as a result. For example, a cruise liner can produce more than 100,000 litres of dirty water just from the toilets on board every day, and almost a million litres of waste water from bathrooms and kitchens. All of this is dumped into the sea. Even worse, every liner dumps about 60 litres of waste that contains harmful chemicals (from things like photography or dry-cleaning facilities) into the sea every day.

Those determined to protect our seas say it's impossible to continue like this. 'Cruise pollution is damaging sea life,' says Jim West, environmental expert. 'The longer we allow this to continue, the worse it is going to get. We need international rules to control the situation,' he added.

Large cruise ships are now carrying over 3,000 passengers on average, and new 'giant' cruise ships which take over 6,000 passengers will very soon be sailing our seas. We need to take action quickly to avoid an international emergency.

B Read the article again. For questions 1-4, choose the correct answer, a, b, or c.

1   What kinds of people choose a holiday on a cruise ship?
    a   people who have a hectic lifestyle and just want to sit quietly on a ship
    b   people who only want to relax, swim and look at the view
    c   people who don't want a boring holiday, but also like to relax

2   How does the writer describe modern cruise ships? As
    a   very large
    b   traditional in style
    c   popular with all people

3   What produces more than 100,000 litres of dirty water every day?
    a   the bathrooms on board a cruise ship
    b   the kitchens on board a cruise ship
    c   the toilets on board a cruise ship

4   What does Jim West say in the article?
    a   new-style giant cruise ships will create fewer problems in international waters
    b   all sea life will die if countries don't get together soon and look for solutions
    c   all countries must get together and try to find solutions to cruise pollution before it's too late

Vocabulary Link

C Complete the table with these words and phrases.

> arrow   battle   canvas   coastline   courage   creative   daughter
> diver   freedom   friendly   helpful   life jacket   patient
> pebbly   pottery   relative   sculpture   studio   sword   watersports

Units 1-4			
Friends and Family	Legends and Heroes	Arts and Crafts	The Sea

Add any other appropriate words you learnt in Units 1-4 to the table.

Grammar Link

D Read the paragraph. For questions 1-8, choose the correct answer, a, b, or c.

Picasso

Pablo Picasso was born in 1881 in Malaga, Spain. Pablo (**1**) _____ in different places, but his favourite was Barcelona. His family (**2**) _____ there in 1895 and Pablo loved the city life. From an early age, Picasso showed great artistic talent. His father was also a painter and realised that his son was very (**3**) _____ . Pablo (**4**) _____ great pictures even as a teenager. In the early 1990s, he moved to Paris. While he (**5**) _____ there he became part of an exciting artistic community and it was a very important time in his artistic and personal life. Other artists had an effect on him, but he was himself very inventive and (**6**) _____ and from early on in his career he had a reputation as an artist who was creating something new and different. Picasso died in 1971 after having lived a very full life. Many people now (**7**) _____ that he is the most important artist of the twentieth century. But one thing is certain: whether you like or dislike his art, almost everybody (**8**) _____ of Pablo Picasso.

1	**a** is growing up	**b**	grew up	**c**	grows up
2	**a** was moving	**b**	moved	**c**	has moved
3	**a** amazing	**b**	kind	**c**	gifted
4	**a** used to draw	**b**	has been drawing	**c**	has drawn
5	**a** has been living	**b**	used to live	**c**	was living
6	**a** original	**b**	boring	**c**	polite
7	**a** are believing	**b**	have believed	**c**	believe
8	**a** heard	**b**	has heard	**c**	hears

Vocabulary Link

A Circle the correct words.

Modern Mobile Phones

In case all you mobile phone (1) owners / populations hadn't already realised, having a brand new, modern mobile phone could just change your whole life. First of all, the new telephones have fantastic designs and lots of amazing features. And, (2) whereas / apart from that, mobile phones are, and always have been, a great method of (3) communication / contact . Take text messages for example: you can send a (4) sticking / winking symbol at someone or simply show that you're surprised! And text messages are (5) popular / different from phone calls because the person you send the message to can keep it and look at it again and again. When I bought my mobile, I hadn't (6) existed / expected to use it much, only in emergencies. But in fact, I (7) daily / hardly ever leave it at home now! I've already downloaded all my music onto it, I have photographs of my friends in it and I send e-mails from it. The addresses and numbers of all my friends are on my phone's memory and I can do everything I'm interested (8) on / in through my mobile phone. How did my parents ever survive without a mobile phone? I'll never understand that.

B Complete the puzzle.

1 Communications are very different _____ – not at all like in the past.
2 He sent me a text message sticking out his _____ at me!
3 Can they really _____ how mobile phones will be used in the future?
4 In the _____ , nobody thought text messages would be popular.
5 Do you use your mobile phone as a _____ organiser?
6 How much did you _____ on your new mobile phone?
7 Bill bought a _____ computer, so he can take it everywhere with him.
8 Does this program protect your computer _____ viruses?
9 How long does the _____ on your mobile phone last?

Now complete the sentence with the word in the coloured squares.

Is it _____ to have a mobile phone with us at all times?

C Complete the sentences with these words.

amazement	disconnected	increase	last	several	sign	touch	users

1 Most teenagers today are mobile phone _____ .

2 Did you see the look of _____ on Mum's face when she saw my mobile phone?

3 Felix gets _____ text messages every hour!

4 There's been an _____ in the sales of video phones.

5 My mobile helps me to stay in _____ with my friends in America.

6 Shelly's learning _____ language because her new boyfriend is deaf.

7 I tried to phone you earlier but I kept getting _____ so I gave up in the end.

8 How long does the battery on your new mobile _____?

Grammar Link

D Complete the paragraph with the correct form of these verbs. Use the Past Perfect Simple.

arrange	break	fall	hope	not expect	not tell	phone	say	send	sit down

A Good Excuse

Jeremy (1) _____ Sally five times that evening to see if she was coming to the party. Although she (2) _____ that she would probably be late home from work, he (3) _____ her to be so late. He (4) _____ just _____ down to think about what to do, when the phone rang. 'Hello,' said Sally, 'I've just got home. I (5) _____ to be home sooner, but I (6) _____ my boss that I had a party to go to and he (7) _____ for the staff to go out to dinner. I went for a little while and then made my excuses. I told them that my aunt (8) _____ me a text message saying that my mother (9) _____ down the stairs and (10) _____ her arm and then I left. Aren't mobiles useful?' she said. 'They can always get you out of a difficult situation!'

E Circle the correct words.

1 By lunchtime, she had invited / invited all her friends to her party.

2 He learnt / had learnt the secret code when he was training to be a spy.

3 She smiled / had smiled at him across the crowded room.

4 They had met / met before, but she couldn't remember where.

5 He recognised / had recognised her voice immediately.

6 She understood him, so he didn't need / hadn't needed to explain anything.

7 They sent / had sent each other an e-mail at exactly the same time.

8 John stuck / had stuck a note on the fridge, so his brother knew he was going to be late.

F Decide which phrase, a or b, completes the second sentence in each pair, so that both sentences have a similar meaning.

1 Nobody understood the expressions that the gang used at that time.
At that time, the gang _____ expressions that nobody understood.
  a had used   **b** used

2 I sent her a letter on Tuesday and she got it on Wednesday.
The letter which I had sent her on Tuesday _____ on Wednesday.
  a had arrived   **b** arrived

3 She waited for two hours to use the computer because her brother was on the Internet.
She _____ the computer after she had waited for two hours for her brother to get off the Internet.
  a used   **b** had used

4 International calls were more difficult to make before satellites were used.
The use of satellites _____ it easier to make international calls.
  a made   **b** had made

5 The teacher learnt sign language and then she started teaching at the school for the deaf.
The teacher started teaching at the school for the deaf after _____ sign language.
  a she learnt   **b** she had learnt

6 After receiving an enormous telephone bill, Sam's dad was really angry.
Sam's dad _____ after he had received an enormous telephone bill.
  a had been really angry   **b** was really angry

7 After writing lots of letters to each other, the pen pals finally met.
The pen pals had written lots of letters to each other before _____ .
  a they had finally met   **b** they finally met

8 They went to buy a mobile phone and then they had lunch.
They had lunch after _____ a mobile phone.
  a they bought   **b** they had bought

G Complete the sentences with the correct form of the verbs in brackets. Use the Past Perfect Simple or the Past Simple.

1 They had spoken to each other many times on the phone before they actually _____ (meet).

2 It _____ (be) more difficult for people to communicate before text messages existed.

3 What would life be like if Alexander Graham Bell _____ (not invent) the telephone?

4 Paul _____ (walk) to the post office and posted a letter.

5 Michael realised something was wrong when his friend _____ (not answer) his messages.

6 The bride's cousin _____ (send) a telegram to the couple on their wedding day.

7 Julia _____ (write) postcards to all her friends by 10 o'clock in the morning.

8 The village high in the mountains _____ (not have) any telephones.

Unit 6   The Animal Kingdom

Vocabulary Link

A Complete the e-mail with these words.

adoption	danger	extinction	fee	living	membership	newsletter	wildlife

---

E-mail

New   Reply   Forward   Print   Delete   Send & Receive

Hi Kevin!

How are you? At last I've found time to write to you!

I'm having a fantastic time working at the **(1)** _____ park. I'm so glad I managed to get a job here. It's a great way to earn a **(2)** _____ . The park is huge and there are quite a few animals here that are in **(3)** _____ of **(4)** _____ .

Anyway, I'm really writing to see if you want to become a member of the *Animal Club* and adopt a wild animal for a year. You'll get a **(5)** _____ card, an **(6)** _____ certificate and a regular **(7)** _____ telling you all about the animals here.

In addition, you'll get an invitation to all our fund-raising events. You just have to pay a small **(8)** _____ of £10 per year.

I hope you decide to join. Write soon and tell me if you're interested. By the way, are you enjoying your new job?

Bye for now.

Rick

B Complete the sentences with these phrasal verbs and phrases.

call off	go on	make up for	run out	set up
take part in		turn into	waste money on	

1 Dad doesn't want me to _____ a new cage for my hamster. He says the old one is fine.

2 We had to _____ the trip to the zoo because of bad weather.

3 They are going to _____ their farm _____ a wildlife park.

4 My brother told me to get off the horse but I wanted to _____ riding.

5 Will the money we've raised for animal welfare _____ soon?

6 Are you going to _____ the local animal welfare campaign?

7 The local government plans to _____ a natural history museum in the city centre.

8 Will we ever _____ the mistakes of the past and help wild animals survive?

C **Complete the words.**

1 This animal can protect you or your property. g _ _ _ | d _ _

2 This is the word for animals which live with people. p _ _ _

3 This is a place where people keep animals or grow food for a living. f _ _ _

4 This person is a doctor who looks after animals. v _ _

5 This is a species of big cat. c _ _ _ | _ _ _

6 This is another word for cows and bulls. c _ _ _ | _ _

7 This is a colourful bird. p _ _ _ | _ _

8 This is the hair that covers some animals' skin. f _ _ | _ _

D **Use the words in capitals at the end of each sentence to make words which fit in the spaces.**

1 Simon wants to help and _____ the African wildlife. *PROTECTION*

2 Sometimes animals die from _____ because they can't find food. *STARVE*

3 I can't believe you _____ with me; of course hunting should be stopped. *AGREE*

4 We must _____ now in order to make a difference in the future. *ACTION*

5 _____ animals are often shot by farmers. *TRAP*

6 Todd's going to join a wildlife _____ when he's got enough money. *ORGANISE*

7 _____ , people still enjoy hunting wild animals. *FORTUNATE*

8 The annual list of _____ species tells us which animals are close to extinction and must be protected. *DANGER*

Grammar Link

E **In each line of this paragraph there is a word that is not needed. Circle the extra word.**

1 Many governments around the world have promised that they will to make

2 special arrangements to protect endangered wildlife. They are going not to create

3 protected areas where these species will are be able to live and hunt in safety.

4 New laws will make them hunting these animals illegal and hunters

5 will going be sent to prison. The sad truth, however, is that

6 this is will have the opposite effect: items such as animal skins, elephant tusks

7 and rhinoceros horns will are be even more desirable and, as a result,

8 people are going to will be prepared to pay more for them.

F Complete the sentences with the correct form of the verbs in brackets. Use the Future Simple or *be going to*.

1 Look at that lion; it _____ (attack) the deer!

2 I think I _____ (send) some money to WWF.

3 Many animals _____ (become) extinct without a natural environment to live and hunt in.

4 We're sure that you _____ (learn) many things from our new wildlife documentary.

5 The government has threatened that it _____ (put) all hunters in prison.

6 My parents are really excited; they _____ (go) on a safari next week.

7 The organisation has made secret plans; it _____ (set) the trapped animals free.

8 Farmers have promised that they _____ (find) other ways of protecting their cattle without killing wild animals.

G Match the beginnings of the sentences to their endings.

Beginnings	Endings
1 They are going	a make hunting illegal.
2 We must do something soon,	b become extinct.
3 They will try to save	c will take the factory owners to court.
4 Lots of our customers are	d to introduce new laws to protect wildlife.
5 The government promises that it will	e going to become extinct.
6 The animal welfare organisation says it	f or certain species will disappear.
7 Judging from the facts and figures, the Indian tiger is	g the African elephant by introducing new laws.
8 Many people think that some endangered species will	h going to go on safari holidays in the summer.

Unit 7 Stepping Out into the World

Vocabulary Link

A Complete the letter with these words.

application	assistant	boss	department	filling	income	touch	unemployment

Dear Helena,

Thanks for your last letter. I'm glad that you've found a job with a good **(1)** _____ which is helping you save some money. I hope you'll be able to afford the new bike that you wanted now.

I haven't made much progress in finding a job. I have sent seven **(2)** _____ forms to different companies but I haven't even got an interview yet. I'm getting sick of **(3)** _____ in forms but I must keep going because **(4)**_____ isn't much fun! There's a job for an office **(5)** _____ in the sales **(6)** _____ of Gregson & Sons; it's advertised in the local paper. I could apply for that, I suppose. It's not my ideal job, but at least I could earn some money. Also, I've heard that the **(7)** _____ is really horrible, so I'm not very keen. I'm also thinking about getting in **(8)** _____ with the Careers Advisory Service at college for some help. What do you think?

Write soon to tell me how you're getting on at work.

Take care,
Joshua

B Complete the words.

1   This takes place in court.   t _ _ _ _ _
2   This gives us information about a college or university.   p _ _ _ _ _ _ _ _ _
3   This is a school book with information about a subject.   t _ _ _ _ _ _ _
4   This is the name for a teacher at university.   l _ _ _ _ _ _ _
5   This person works for another person.   e _ _ _ _ _ _ _ _
6   This is something that is unusual or not normal.   s _ _ _ _ _ _ _
7   This is the name for a very rich person.   m _ _ _ _ _ _ _ _ _ _
8   This is the money that professional people get for doing their job.   s _ _ _ _ _

C Circle the correct words.

1   My job is very normal / unusual ; I'm an astronaut.
2   People working in the medical profession / career usually earn a good salary.
3   Part of his job involves listening to long cases in office / court .
4   Take a notebook / reading list with you so you can write down things you need to remember.
5   Is Mr Fenwick one of the workmen / partners or is he just the manager?
6   We are going to my sister's graduation / degree ceremony next Friday.
7   I'm finding the work here rather dull / glad . My old job was a lot more exciting.
8   Do I get paid extra for running all your terms / errands ?

Grammar Link

D Circle the correct words.

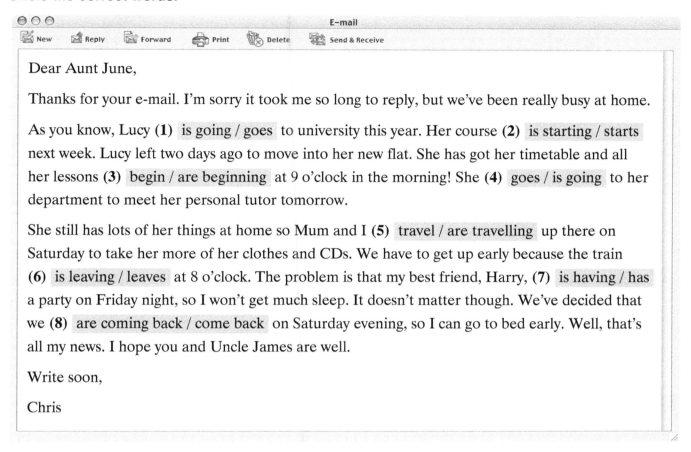

Dear Aunt June,

Thanks for your e-mail. I'm sorry it took me so long to reply, but we've been really busy at home.

As you know, Lucy **(1)** is going / goes to university this year. Her course **(2)** is starting / starts next week. Lucy left two days ago to move into her new flat. She has got her timetable and all her lessons **(3)** begin / are beginning at 9 o'clock in the morning! She **(4)** goes / is going to her department to meet her personal tutor tomorrow.

She still has lots of her things at home so Mum and I **(5)** travel / are travelling up there on Saturday to take her more of her clothes and CDs. We have to get up early because the train **(6)** is leaving / leaves at 8 o'clock. The problem is that my best friend, Harry, **(7)** is having / has a party on Friday night, so I won't get much sleep. It doesn't matter though. We've decided that we **(8)** are coming back / come back on Saturday evening, so I can go to bed early. Well, that's all my news. I hope you and Uncle James are well.

Write soon,

Chris

E Complete the paragraph with the correct form of the verbs in brackets. Use the Present Simple or the Present Continuous.

Looking Forward to Summer

I **(1)** _____ (leave) school soon. I'm very lucky because I have already found a job which **(2)** _____ (start) in five months' time. That actually means that I **(3)** _____ (have) two months in the summer to do whatever I want. So, in two weeks I **(4)** _____ (go) to Miami, Florida to visit my friend. My flight **(5)** _____ (leave) at 9 o'clock in the morning on July 1st and **(6)** _____ (arrive) in America at 2 o'clock in the afternoon local time. They are five hours behind London, but the flight takes about ten hours. I have never been on such a long flight before, so I **(7)** _____ (take) my MP3 player and a good book with me. My friend, Julie, **(8)** _____ (come) to the airport to meet me. It's her birthday that day, so she **(9)** _____ (have) a big dinner party. I am really looking forward to it, but first I must pay for the flight. Tomorrow I **(10)** _____ (go) into town to do just that!

F Write a sentence for each of the situations. Use the Present Simple or the Present Continuous.

1   the meeting / start / at 10 am tomorrow

_____

_____

2   school / start / on 1st September

_____

_____

3   the businessman's flight / take off / at 6 am / tomorrow

_____

_____

4   Helen / visit / the new college / on Friday

_____

_____

5   the art students / hold / an art exhibition / next week

_____

_____

6   They / have / a leaving party / for Sandra / on Monday

_____

_____

G Decide which phrase, a or b, completes the second sentence in each pair, so that both sentences have a similar meaning.

1   The timetable says that all maths lectures start at 11.15 am.
    The timetable says that all maths lectures _____ at 11.15 am.
    a   are   **b**   are being

2   I must catch the train just before nine o' clock tomorrow morning.
    My train _____ just before nine o' clock tomorrow morning.
    a   leaves   **b**   is leaving

3   There will be a new manager at work tomorrow.
    A new manager _____ at work tomorrow.
    a   starts   **b**   is starting

4   The college will sell some of its old books next month.
    The college _____ some of its old books next month.
    a   is selling   **b**   sells

5   You will have a higher salary after you have worked here for six months.
    Your salary _____ after you have worked here for six months.
    a   is increasing   **b**   increases

6   Mr Smith is going to be our new supervisor from June 1st.
    Mr Smith _____ us from June 1st.
    a   supervises   **b**   is supervising

7   There are exams for all biology students in January.
    All biology students _____ exams in January.
    a   sit   **b**   are sitting

8   The students are going to an art exhibition with their lecturer tomorrow.
    The lecturer _____ her students to an art exhibition tomorrow.
    a   takes   **b**   is taking

Unit 8 Leisure

Vocabulary Link

A Complete the letter with these words and phrases.

among   boat   cages   drive-through   fed   join in   safari   wild

Dear Trudy,

I'm having a brilliant time here at the (1) _____ park. I wish you were here!

I've seen loads of different and unusual (2) _____ animals, and the great thing is that they aren't in (3) _____ like they are at the zoo. Even when the animals are a bit dangerous, you can still be (4) _____ them from the safety of your car because it's a (5) _____ park.

It's great because you can (6) _____ with what's going on at the park. This morning, I (7) _____ the sea lions for an hour before I had a quick bite to eat myself at the café by the river.

Later on, we're going on a (8) _____ trip on the river and I hope we'll see the crocodiles!

You'd love it here - I hope you get the chance to come one day.

See you soon.

Maggie

B Circle the odd one out.

1	exact	approximate	correct	accurate
2	plenty	lots of	a bit	a number of
3	climbing	abseiling	bungee jumping	adventure weekend
4	snack	bite to eat	drink	food
5	kiosk	café	restaurant	park

C Circle the correct words.

1 Mike's favourite leisure / excitement activity is bungee jumping.

2 The wildlife park covers about 500 places / acres .

3 You'll learn some new techniques / facilities for extreme sports on the course.

4 We saw a huge territory / variety of animals I'd never seen before.

5 There's a new nature / sports reserve opening near us next month.

6 It was well after eleven when they got home from the day out at the game / pet park.

7 Brian learnt several basic / tiring survival techniques on the weekend course.

8 Hey! Let's do something different for a change / chance and go bungee jumping!

D Complete the crossword.

Across

3 These sports can be dangerous.

5 cycling

7 a kind or kinds of animal

8 a short holiday

9 a wild animal which looks like a dog

10 animals that live with people

Down

1 a pink bird with long legs

2 coloured birds that can talk

4 a very basic kind of building

6 people who teach you on courses

Now rearrange the letters in the coloured squares to make words to complete the sentence.

A _____ _____ is a great place to visit!

Grammar Link

E In each line of this paragraph there is a word that is not needed. Circle the extra word.

1 During the summer holidays one year, we were decided to go camping. None

2 of us had been going camping before, so we were excited about trying something new.

3 We began our journey early on Saturday morning and we did travelled by train to

4 the Welsh countryside. We had be found a campsite on the map before we left that

5 was within walking distance of the train station. We were arrived at 2 o'clock and after

6 we had paid for our site we had started putting up our tent. None of us had

7 been done it before and my friend John managed to hurt his thumb and I

8 couldn't stop laughing. We have had planned to do many things during our break,

9 like biking, swimming and rock-climbing. However, as soon as we had done finished

10 with the tent, it started raining; and it didn't not stop. We have never been camping again!

F Match the beginnings of the sentences to their endings.

Beginnings	Endings
1 Paul has already decided that	a at 3 o'clock on Sundays.
2 While Jane was playing tennis,	b this winter in the Alps.
3 The teenage girl broke her leg	c he is going to try bungee jumping.
4 Is the karate team having a tournament	d but now I send her e-mails.
5 The local Internet café closes	e her brother was doing his homework.
6 They have been camping in the forest	f while she was skiing on Friday afternoon.
7 I used to send my cousin letters,	g next Saturday?
8 Her son is going to start snowboarding	h for the past three weeks.

G Decide which phrase, a or b, completes the second sentence in each pair, so that both sentences have a similar meaning.

1 We have decided to go camping next weekend.
We _____ camping next weekend.
a are going   b had gone

2 I don't go to the Internet café now that I have my own PC.
I _____ go to the Internet café before I had my own PC.
a used to   b didn't

3 We played a game of tennis and then we went for a swim.
We went for a swim after we _____ a game of tennis.
a had played   b were playing

4 The local council has promised to build a new sports centre in our area.
The local council has promised that it _____ a new sports centre in our area.
a is building   b will build

5 Liz started judo three months ago. She loves it!
Liz _____ judo for three months. She loves it!
a had learnt   b has been learning

6 The park is a popular meeting place for teenagers on Saturdays.
Many teenagers _____ each other in the park on Saturdays.
a meet   b are meeting

7 I have arranged to take my niece to a safari park next weekend.
I _____ my niece to a safari park next weekend.
a will take   b am going to take

8 It's a long time since Paul rode his mountain bike.
Paul _____ his mountain bike for a long time.
a wasn't riding   b hasn't ridden

Reading Link

A Read the article quickly and find out what an employment agency does.

JOINING THE WORLD OF WORK

In three months, Lisa Mills leaves school, and then she will have to look for work. Like so many people her age, Lisa will have her first job-hunting experience in a world where not many jobs are available. Furthermore, there are many people looking for jobs who have qualifications such as university degrees, which Lisa does not have. Although she is looking forward to beginning her new life, Lisa is nervous about the difficulties of finding a job.

This is why she has decided to go to an employment agency. (An employment agency matches people's skills and qualifications with the needs of employers.) Hopefully, this will mean that she won't have to spend months looking through newspaper advertisements in order to find a job. Although Lisa has decided not to go to university, she hopes that her strong computer skills will make it easy for the agency to find a job for her.

However, Lisa knows that it will not be easy to find a job, especially as she wants one that she will enjoy; she would like to find something that can become a career in the future and that can help her grow as a person. Although earning money is an important part of work, she, like many people, feels that this alone is not enough to keep her happy if she doesn't actually like the job itself. As Lisa says, 'It is very important to enjoy what you do. After all, our working life lasts for more than forty years.'

B Read the article again. For questions 1-5, choose the correct answer, a, b or c.

1 What is going to happen to Lisa?
 a She has exams in three months.
 b She starts work in three months.
 c She must look for work in three months.

2 How does Lisa feel about looking for a job?
 a excited and happy
 b sad and worried
 c excited but also worried

3 Why is Lisa going to an employment agency?
 a It might make things easier for her.
 b It is the only way to find work.
 c She cannot find a good job.

4 What does Lisa think about getting a job?
 a It doesn't matter which job it is.
 b She wants to find something she likes.
 c It won't be difficult.

5 What does Lisa feel is important about work?
 a It must be enjoyable.
 b It must be better than university.
 c It must pay a lot of money.

Vocabulary Link

C Complete the table with these words and phrases.

adventure weekend   boat trip   cattle   climbing   day out   e-mail
employer   endangered   extinct   graduation   hunt   lecture   mobile   Morse code
occupation   prospectus   sign language   sports centre   text message   wildlife

Units 5-8			
Communication	The Animal Kingdom	Stepping Out into the World	Leisure

Add any other appropriate words you learnt in Units 5-8 to the table.

Grammar Link

D Read the paragraph. For questions 1-8, choose the correct answer, a, b, or c.

Our Closest Relatives

In Africa, gorillas and chimpanzees are losing their forest habitat, which humans (1) _____ for many years. Furthermore, many of these animals live in countries which are in the middle of wars that (2) _____ for a very long time. To make the problem even worse, hunting animals for meat is something that produces a lot of money in West and Central Africa. Some wildlife organisations (3) _____ to create programmes to save these animals, but they soon discovered that it was impossible. This (4) _____ tragic results for the animals very soon. The organisations still (5) _____ to try to create a programme to save these animals, but they must be able to get to the areas and have the support and help of the local community. They (6) _____ animals all over the world for many years now, but it is education that (7) _____ the biggest difference. Humans (8) _____ only of themselves for far too long.

1	a had destroyed	b have been destroying	c destroys
2	a continued	b had continued	c are going to continue
3	a had hoped	b are hoping	c hopes
4	a will have	b had had	c has
5	a has been wanting	b want	c had wanted
6	a are protecting	b have been protecting	c had protected
7	a had made	b will make	c used to make
8	a had thought	b will think	c have been thinking

Vocabulary Link

A Complete the paragraph with these words.

afford   bank   goods   into   loans   save   take   up   value   wealthy

Money Management

I didn't come from a (1) _____ family but I was always taught that it's important to (2) _____ for a rainy day. When I was young, my mum used to pay some money (3) _____ the (4) _____ for me. I soon learned the (5) _____ of money. When I was older I would walk round the shops and look at all the (6) _____ for sale, seeing what I could (7) _____ . If I saw something I really wanted, I used to save (8) _____ for it. Then I'd (9) _____ my money out of the bank and go and buy it. I think that's what more people should do today, instead of getting (10) _____ all the time!

B Circle the correct words.

1 Some people believe money was the worst invention / discovery ever!

2 Don't forget to take some local currency / cheques when you go abroad.

3 I've got some cash / credit cards , but not enough to buy this MP3 player.

4 As soon as she got the money, she went to the bank to withdraw / deposit it.

5 They've got some old Chinese paper banknotes / coins in the National Museum.

6 Grandad was very poor / proud and never had a lot of money to spend.

7 I think rich people have more opportunities / developments in life than the poor.

8 China produced / printed the first metal coins.

9 James already owes / stole a lot of money to the bank, so I don't think they'll give him another loan.

10 They use machines in lots of shops now to check that banknotes aren't creations / forgeries .

C Complete the sentences with the correct form of these verbs and phrases.

| change into |
| come to |
| hand over |
| make out of |
| pay back |
| pay for |
| stamped on |
| use as |

1 Ted bought a laptop and a printer and the total price only _____ £600!

2 I need to _____ some pounds _____ dollars.

3 Could I _____ this book in euros, please?

4 Some ancient coins had the heads of gods _____ them.

5 Thanks for the loan; I'll _____ you _____ next week.

6 The bank manager _____ the money _____ to the robber.

7 In 1000 BC, the Chinese _____ cowrie shells _____ bronze and copper.

8 People _____ lots of different things _____ money before coins and banknotes were invented.

Grammar Link

D Circle the correct words.

1 The news last night was / were all about the economy.

2 She paid £100 to have her hair / hairs cut.

3 That luggage is nice, but it's / they're too expensive.

4 She gave me an / some advice on how to save money.

5 In the museum, we saw a / some shells like the ones the Chinese used as money.

6 I went to the bank to ask for an / some information.

7 They know he robbed the bank because the money was / were found in his home.

8 We bought a / some lovely cheese to have after dinner tonight.

E Match the beginnings of the sentences to their endings.

Beginnings		Endings	
1	They told me that there weren't	a	United States of America.
2	The money you asked for	b	a new family car.
3	She lost all her money in the	c	is on the kitchen table.
4	The Harrisons want to buy	d	some forged banknotes.
5	At the local bank they discovered	e	Egyptian holiday.
6	Your grandfather's old coins	f	the house they bought in London.
7	He spent his money on a(n)	g	are under your bed.
8	The Johnsons paid £400,000 for	h	any forged banknotes.

F Decide which phrase, a or b, completes the second sentence in each pair, so that both sentences have a similar meaning.

1 He doesn't know anything about the robbery.
   He doesn't _____ of the robbery.
   a have any knowledge   **b** have some knowledge

2 The table and chairs they bought were very expensive.
   The furniture _____ very expensive.
   a they bought were   **b** they bought was

3 The price of salt has increased.
   Salt _____ than it used to be.
   a is more expensive   **b** are more expensive

4 The chocolate she bought was delicious, but very expensive.
   She bought _____ chocolate, but it was very expensive.
   a any delicious   **b** some delicious

5 They have cheap fruit at that supermarket.
   The fruit they have at _____ cheap.
   a that supermarket is   **b** that supermarket are

6 They were too late to go to the bank because of the terrible traffic.
   The traffic _____ were too late to go to the bank.
   a was terrible so they   **b** were terrible so they

7 They gave her forged notes at the bank.
   The notes which they gave her _____ forged.
   a at the bank was   **b** at the bank were

8 Notes are lighter than coins.
   Coins _____ than notes.
   a is heavier   **b** are heavier

G Complete the text with a/an, the, some or – .

Money Wise

My brother Sam and I are twins. For our 16th birthday, Mum gave us **(1)** _____ money to spend instead of buying us presents. Sam decided to spend his on a ticket for **(2)** _____ latest production at **(3)** _____ Gleeve Theatre and **(4)** _____ meal. I laughed and told him that he was wasting his money; but I couldn't think of what to buy, so I put mine in my jeans pocket and went to do **(5)** _____ homework.

On the way home from **(6)** _____ school the next day, I had **(7)** _____ idea. I decided that I would buy **(8)** _____ black boots that I had seen the week before. I ran home to get the money out of my pocket, only to find that Mum had put my jeans in the washing machine! I was so upset that I couldn't speak. I went to my bedroom to get ready to play **(9)** _____ basketball, but when I got there I saw the money on my bed, next to a note from Sam! **(10)** _____ note said, 'I saw you putting this in your pocket and took it out again just in time! Next time, look after your own money before you tell others they are wasting theirs!' I was so happy that I promised never to laugh at Sam again.

Unit 10 Emergency Services

Vocabulary Link

A Complete the e-mail with these words.

accident	ambulance	calm	chaotic	drip	nurse	road	uniform

E-mail

New   Reply   Forward   Print   Delete   Send & Receive

Hi Wendy,

Thanks for your e-mail. I'm glad you are well.

I've just finished my first month as a student **(1)** _____ in the **(2)** _____ and emergency department of City Hospital. I'm really enjoying it, but I'm very busy. I've had to learn lots of new things, like how to change a patient's **(3)** _____ . There's a lot happening here and it's sometimes very **(4)** _____ as you can imagine, especially when we get people who've been in **(5)** _____ accidents of course.

The other people here are really friendly, and everyone works very hard. The **(6)** _____ drivers have an important job, and I'm quite interested in training to become one in the future. I've discovered that I'm very good at staying **(7)** _____ in emergencies.

Anyway, I start work in half an hour, so I'd better go and put my **(8)** _____ on.

Take care and write soon with all your news.

Grace

B Complete the words.

1   This person helps swimmers in danger in the sea.   l _ _ _ _ _ _ _ _

2   You call this if you see a fire.   f _ _ _ b _ _ _ _ _ _

3   These help you to walk if you have injured your leg.   c _ _ _ _ _ _ _

4   People are carried into hospital on one of these if they can't walk or sit.   s _ _ _ _ _ _ _ _

5   People sometimes get this when they stay on the beach for too long.   s _ _ _ _ _ _ _

6   The police can help you in this kind of situation.   e _ _ _ _ _ _ _ _

7   This is what your medical information is written on in a hospital.   c _ _ _ _

8   You must know this to join any of the emergency services.   f _ _ _ _ a _ _

C Match the beginnings of the sentences to their endings.

Beginnings

1 Firefighters must be alert in difficult
2 Chris went on a first-aid
3 Lifeguards have to be physically
4 I think there is a free training
5 They all waited at the scene of the
6 Sam didn't know he was colour
7 Luckily, John was a strong
8 You must tell the emergency services your post

Endings

a code so they can get to you quickly.
b accident until the ambulance arrived.
c blind until he took a test for the fire brigade.
d situations so that they can help people.
e fit and strong.
f course for lifeguards next week.
g course as part of his training.
h swimmer so he got back to the beach without a problem.

D Use the words in capitals at the end of each sentence to make words which fit in the spaces.

1 I can't imagine that being a rescue worker could ever be _____ . *BORE*
2 Greg's just started working as a _____ ambulance driver. *TRAIN*
3 Of all the emergency _____ , I think the fire brigade has the most dangerous job. *SERVI*
4 This dog has been _____ trained to rescue swimmers from the sea. *SPECIAL*
5 There was a huge _____ and then the building collapsed. *EXPLODE*
6 If you have the _____ to keep calm in an emergency, you could be a policeman. *ABLE*
7 I love being a lifeguard. It's the most _____ job in the world! *EXCITE*
8 Fred could never be a fireman. He can't lift heavy _____ . *WEIGH*
9 Do you _____ that lifeguard? It's John! *RECOGNITION*
10 _____ is the most important quality if you're a nurse. *PATIENT*

Grammar Link

E Decide which phrase, a or b, completes the second sentence in each pair so that both sentences have a similar meaning.

1 Firefighters need to be very brave when they are saving people.
   Firefighters _____ be very brave when they are saving people.
   a must   b can

2 It isn't necessary to be tall to be a firefighter.
   You _____ be tall to be a firefighter.
   a don't have to   b mustn't

3 Do we have to call the police?
   _____ we call the police?
   a Can   b Must

4 You are not allowed to get on the boat without a life jacket on.
   You _____ get on the boat without a life jacket on.
   a mustn't   b don't have to

5 John wasn't able to decide if he wanted to be an ambulance driver or not.
   John _____ decide if he wanted to be an ambulance driver or not.
   a didn't have to   b couldn't

6 The police needed to rush to the crime scene.
   The police _____ rush to the crime scene.
   a had to   b could

7 The doctors saved the patient's life.
   The doctors _____ save the patient's life.
   a were able to   b must

8 The old rescue helicopter couldn't fly when it was very windy.
   The old rescue helicopter _____ fly when it was very windy.
   a wasn't able to   b didn't have to

F Circle the correct words.

Staying Calm Saves Lives

Whenever there is a big disaster like an earthquake, for example, the emergency services
(1) can / have to act as quickly as possible. The people who work for these services **(2)** could / must
be very well trained and they have to **(3)** can / be able to stay calm. This is also true for the people
around the scene who want to help. Anybody who **(4)** mustn't / can't stay calm can create an even
more dangerous situation than the one that already **(5)** has to / can be dealt with.

The emergency services also need the help of animals to do the things that a human being
(6) couldn't / isn't able to do. Dogs, for example, **(7)** must / are able to find people who are trapped
under collapsed buildings much more quickly than humans **(8)** have to / can . These people **(9)** can / must
be found as quickly as possible, so that rescue teams **(10)** can / mustn't act immediately and save lives.

G Write a sentence for each of the situations. Use the correct form of can, must, have to or
be able to. More than one answer may be possible.

1 the firefighter / climb / a ladder /
to save / the girl / yesterday

_____

_____

_____

2 the rescue team don't want /
helpers / who / not / stay calm

_____

_____

_____

3 rescue workers / not / go / to
dangerous sites / on their own

_____

_____

_____

4 ambulances / always / get / to
hospital / quickly

_____

_____

_____

5 you / not be / a doctor /
to save / someone's life

_____

_____

_____

6 all fit men and women / join /
the emergency services

_____

_____

_____

Unit 11 Shopping

Vocabulary Link

A Complete the text with these phrases.

charge for
credit cards
designer clothes
good value
mail order catalogue
make up my mind
shopping trip
spend money on

Debbie's Dream

Imagine if you could go on the (1) _____ of your dreams! Where would you go and what would you do? Well, Debbie knows exactly what she wants to do.

'I dream of going to New York with at least ten (2) _____ to do my shopping!' says Debbie. 'Right now I do most of my shopping from a (3) _____ because I haven't got a lot of money. But my dream is to go to one of those huge department stores in the USA and (4) _____ all the (5) _____ I want! I don't know how much they (6) _____ things like that in the USA, and I don't imagine everything would be what my mum would call (7) _____ , but I don't care! And anyway, I might be lucky and find some things cheaper there, so I might even get a few bargains. The problem might be that I won't be able to (8) _____ about what I want! But just think what fun it would be to try on all those fantastic clothes! I know it's only a dream, but maybe one day it will come true!'

B Circle the correct words.

1   It's not a good idea to write a cheque if you don't have any money in your bank   amount / account .

2   Frances has found some brilliant Internet   sites / shops   for buying clothes.

3   We queued for hours outside the shop so we could find the best clothes in the   sales / bargains .

4   You don't have to pay any   postage / customers   if you buy from this mail-order catalogue.

5   If my sister doesn't like the jeans I've bought her, can I have a   transfer / refund ?

6   I need a few things from the   auction / shopping centre   – can you get them while you're there?

7   Have you ever   ordered / paid   food from a supermarket online?

8   Have you seen the   shiny / brilliant   new sports shop that's opened in town?

9   Did you   spot / mark   the fantastic offers on the second floor?

10   Shopping on the Internet isn't   luxurious / risky   if you're careful.

C Label the pictures.

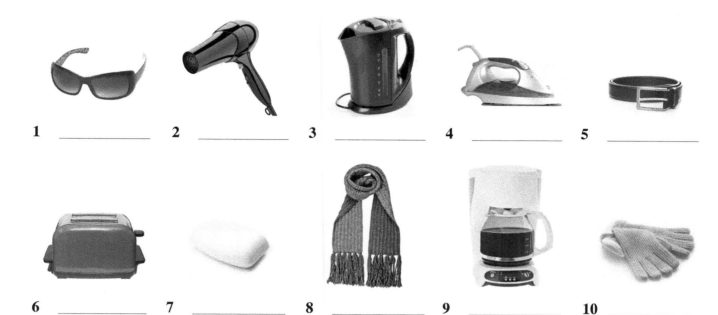

1 _____
2 _____
3 _____
4 _____
5 _____

6 _____
7 _____
8 _____
9 _____
10 _____

Grammar Link

D Circle the correct words.

1 There were a lot of people at the music shop and they all / both wanted concert tickets.

2 He spent a few / a lot of money on clothes yesterday.

3 We shop at this supermarket, but either / neither of us likes it.

4 They looked in all the shops, but neither / none of them had what they wanted.

5 I think I'll buy both / all the red T-shirt and the green T-shirt.

6 Paul went to buy a DVD player, but they only had a little / a few to choose from.

7 Olivia didn't like neither / either of the two dresses.

8 They wanted to go shopping, but they only had a few / a little time.

E In each sentence there is a word that is not needed. Circle the extra word.

1 Both Harry and Sally bought all new clothes yesterday.

2 Tom didn't like either of both the games his parents had bought him.

3 She tried on two T-shirts, but neither of them fitted her either.

4 He wanted to buy a few music video, but the ones he liked had all been sold.

5 Sarah spent a lot of money on none sweets yesterday.

6 They both wanted to buy the blue car, but neither their daughters liked the red one.

7 They are all going to buy few books tomorrow.

8 Bill had a little money to spend on lots presents.

F Circle the correct words.

To Shop or not to Shop?

Paul and Anne were tired and **(1)** neither / either was in a good mood, so they **(2)** all / both wanted to do something that would make them feel better. Jane suggested that they go shopping for clothes and CDs. She said that **(3)** both / all of the shops had sales on, so if **(4)** neither / either of them found something they liked, they could save a **(5)** few / little money. Paul said that he had gone shopping a **(6)** lot of / few days earlier and that **(7)** either / all of the shops were full of rubbish! **(8)** Neither / None of them had anything interesting to look at. So, they stayed at home and watched a DVD instead.

G Write a sentence for each of the situations. Use one of these determiners for each situation.

a few	a little	a lot of	both	either	neither

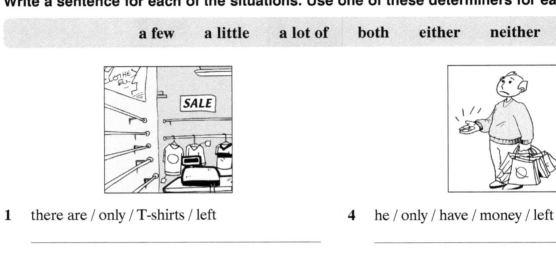

1   there are / only / T-shirts / left

_____

_____

4   he / only / have / money / left

_____

_____

2   there are / people / at the shops

_____

_____

5   she / want / buy / jacket / coat

_____

_____

3   the shirts / fit / him

_____

_____

6   shops / open

_____

_____

Unit 12 Space

Vocabulary Link

A Complete the interview with these words.

| conditions | Earth | galaxy | humans | lake | life | oxygen | planets | scientist | survive |

Questions about Space

Interviewer: Henry, can you tell me the most interesting thing about being a **(1)** _____ who studies space?

Henry: Well, of course, it's very exciting to find out if there's **(2)** _____ anywhere else in the **(3)** _____ apart from on **(4)** _____ . That's the most important question we're looking at these days. But in my job, everything's exciting, to be honest. It's great to learn about the **(5)** _____ that exist on other **(6)** _____ , the average temperature for example, and how much **(7)** _____ there is. We can get an idea of how likely it is that **(8)** _____ like you and me could **(9)** _____ there.

Interviewer: And what project are you working on at the moment?

Henry: I'm studying the ice on the moon. We've already found enough to make a **(10)** _____ of at least 10 square kilometres with a depth of 10 metres. This is important because one day people might be able to use this water to live on the moon.

Interviewer: Well, good luck with your work. It was nice to talk to you.

Henry: It was my pleasure.

B Complete the words.

1 This makes things fall when you drop them.   g _ _ _ _ _ _

2 This word means under the surface of the earth.   u _ _ _ _ _ _ _ _ _ _

3 This is the beginning of a space rocket's journey into space.   l _ _ _ _ _

4 The Earth does this round the sun.   o _ _ _ _ _

5 We read these to find out how to do something.   i _ _ _ _ _ _ _ _ _ _ _

6 This is a thousand million.   b _ _ _ _ _ _

7 These make up the air we breathe.   g _ _ _ _

8 The Phoenix Mars Lander was sent to do this on the red planet.   e _ _ _ _ _ _

C Complete the puzzle.

1 Wherever we live, we have to have _____ to breathe.

2 Neil Armstrong was the first _____ to walk on the moon.

3 After Earth, _____ has the best conditions for life.

4 It's fun to look at some of the planets through a _____ – it makes them look bigger.

5 Some specialists, or _____ , know a lot about all the planets.

6 There's no _____ that life exists on other planets.

7 Without oxygen, humans couldn't _____ .

8 Air and water are the _____ for life.

9 The _____ is huge and all the galaxies are in it.

10 If there was some real _____ , I'd believe in aliens!

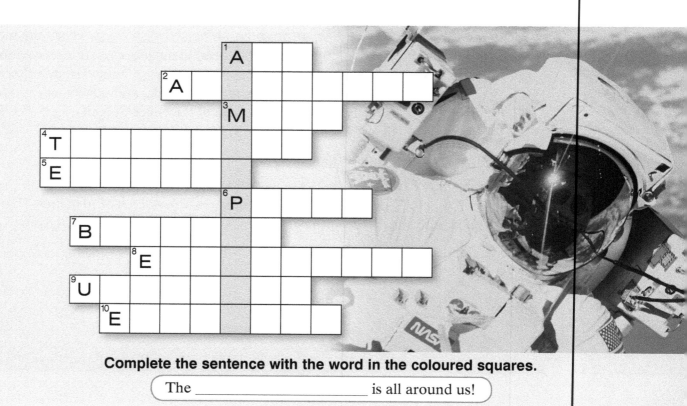

Complete the sentence with the word in the coloured squares.

The _____ is all around us!

D Use the words in capitals at the end of each sentence to make words which fit in the spaces.

1 A week in space really would be a very _____ holiday.   *DIFFERENCE*

2 Is there a _____ that we could live on another planet?   *POSSIBLE*

3 Astronauts must have a medical _____ before they go into space.   *EXAMINE*

4 The exact age of Earth is _____ , but scientists are trying to find out.   *KNOW*

5 If you lived on Mars, all your _____ would be very different.   *SURROUND*

6 There are quite a lot of _____ between Mars and Earth.   *SIMILAR*

7 The air we breathe is made from a _____ of different gases.   *MIX*

8 What did the _____ say about the atmosphere on Mars?   *PHYSICS*

Grammar Link

E Match the beginnings of the sentences to their endings.

  Beginnings

  1 If humans went to live on another planet,

  2 If we found another planet to live on,

  3 If we had the time to go,

  4 If an astronaut visited Mars,

  5 If aliens arrived on Earth,

  6 Some people say that if we looked at the stars,

  Endings

  a we would have to treat it with respect.

  b he would become very famous on Earth.

  c we would all be very scared.

  d we would visit NASA.

  e we would see what our future holds.

  f they would probably destroy that one, too.

F Complete the sentences with the correct form of the verbs in brackets.

1 If I saw a UFO, I _____ (try) to take a photograph of it.

2 If we looked after Earth, we _____ (not have to) look elsewhere for a place to live.

3 What would happen if a meteorite _____ (crash) into Earth?

4 Peter says that if he went into space, he _____ (visit) Saturn.

5 If we continue exploring space, we _____ (discover) how the universe began.

6 If scientists found water on another planet, they _____ (look) for some form of life.

7 If we travelled at the speed of light, we _____ (reach) other planets very quickly.

8 There would be much less hunger and disease if we _____ (not waste) so much money on space travel.

G Circle the correct words.

Space Exploration: Is It Worth It?

There are many politicians and citizens who believe that if we spent less on space exploration, we **(1)** would / will be able to use the money to solve problems on this planet. And if we manage to solve the problems on this planet, we **(2)** wouldn't / won't need to look for somewhere else to live. If we **(3)** considered / consider how much has been spent on space travel, we will be horrified to discover that it amounts to billions of dollars! If countries like the USA used this money for other purposes, they **(4)** will / would help solve problems like poverty, homelessness and unemployment. Others argue that if we **(5)** continue / continued to explore space, we will discover useful sources of energy for our planet. However, if we don't treat the Earth's resources with care and respect, we **(6)** won't / wouldn't treat another planet's resources with respect, either. If we actually **(7)** protect / protected our own environment, we wouldn't need new sources of energy, and if we respected this planet, we **(8)** would / will spend the time and money on making it even more beautiful than it already is!

Reading Link

A Read the dialogue quickly and find at least three things that Adele does to make customers feel happy.

Customer Service

Interviewer: Adele, what do you think is the most important thing about your job as a salesperson?

Adele: I think these days it's definitely customer service.

Interviewer: **1** [ ]

Adele: Well, it's really about making sure that the customer is happy and that he or she is getting the kind of help or attention he or she wants.

Interviewer: I see. Is it like the old saying 'the customer is always right'?

Adele: **2** [ ]

Interviewer: So what sort of things do you do to make the customer happy?

Adele: Oh, sometimes it's simple things like just being polite or smiling at them. **3** [ ] It can also be helping them pack the things they have bought or carrying them out to the car. Things like that. And I think it's also about speaking to the customer the way you would like to be spoken to yourself in a shop.

Interviewer: **4** [ ] I must say, I do think some salespeople can be rude at times.

Adele: Well, I'm sure you won't find that at the shop where I work. Not now we've all had customer service training!

B There are four sentences missing from the dialogue. Read through it again and choose from sentences A-E the one which fits each gap. There is one extra sentence that you do not need to use.

A Other times it might be dealing with a complaint.

B That's an interesting idea.

C Can you explain what that means?

D And how many people like that do you see each day?

E Yes, even when they're wrong!

Vocabulary Link

C Complete the table with these words and phrases.

> accident   ambulance   atmosphere   auction   bargain   currency   customer
> fire brigade   forgery   galaxy   gravity   loan   patient
> poor   queue   sales   stretcher   telescope   universe   wealthy

Units 9-12			
Money	**Emergency Services**	**Shopping**	**Space**

Add any other appropriate words you learnt in Units 9-12 to the table.

Grammar Link

D Read the paragraph. For questions 1-8, choose the correct answer, a, b or c.

A New Idea?

If you visit any major cities in the world today, you **(1)** _____ see that **(2)** _____ shopping malls are being built everywhere. The idea of the shopping mall is that shoppers **(3)** _____ find everything they need in one place and under one roof. But the shopping mall is not a new idea. What may be described as **(4)** _____ first shopping mall was built, and still exists, in the city of Aleppo in **(5)** _____ Syria. It is **(6)** _____ enormous indoor market which was built around 637 AD. It was, and still is, a great bazaar called a *souq*. More than eight kilometres of narrow stone passages are connected under its roof with hundreds of stalls selling all kinds of things. You can buy **(7)** _____ gold or exotic spices, pure olive oil or perfumes from all over the world. When it was built, this great bazaar had water fountains, places to eat and baths called hammam, where people could relax, because they **(8)** _____ travel great distances by horse or camel to come to the bazaar. And all this could be done while the enormous roof protected you from the cold in winter and the incredible heat in summer.

1	**a**	would	**b**	could	**c**	will
2	**a**	a little	**b**	a lot of	**c**	a few
3	**a**	could	**b**	couldn't	**c**	can
4	**a**	the	**b**	a	**c**	an
5	**a**	–	**b**	the	**c**	a
6	**a**	the	**b**	an	**c**	a
7	**a**	some	**b**	a few	**c**	all
8	**a**	must	**b**	will	**c**	had to

Unit 13 Ambitions

Vocabulary Link

A Circle the correct words.

> *Dear* Music World,
>
> *I'm writing to you about my big* **(1)** *ambition / situation – to be a singer! I thought you might be able to give me some* **(2)** *experience / advice .*
>
> *People tell me that I'm already an* **(3)** *imaginative / excellent singer, and I've been to* **(4)** *primary / evening classes to have some special training. The teachers there have always given me good* **(5)** *marks / comments (almost 100%!), and said nice things about me in the* **(6)** *reports / compositions they have written. But my parents, who are retired and don't have very modern ideas, say I'll never be a famous singer. I* **(7)** *apply / intend to prove them wrong!*
>
> *I really want to succeed. Can you help me to* **(8)** *achieve / manage my dream?*
>
> *Yours hopefully,*
>
> *Susannah Stevens*

B Underline the wrong word in each of the sentences and write the correct word.

1   Jeff and David have been friends since second school.   _____

2   Did you always take good marks at school?   _____

3   James would like to make research when he leaves university.   _____

4   Helen is in the third class at high school.   _____

5   The students had to learn the poem from heart.   _____

6   If you can't receive criticism, your work will not improve.   _____

7   He applied in college and was accepted.   _____

8   It didn't take her long to find the ropes at work.   _____

C Complete the puzzle.

1 Justin's a great _____ ; he's got a lovely voice.

2 Now that Grace has trained as a _____ , she can give you advice about the law.

3 Their dad's a _____ , so he makes all the tables and chairs in their house.

4 The _____ who did Jane's operation had 10 years' experience.

5 Why don't you get a job as a _____ in the Italian restaurant for the summer?

6 I wonder how many articles a _____ writes every day?

7 It's not surprising that Brian's a famous _____ ; he was always good at science at school.

8 Wendy's biology _____ didn't encourage her much at school.

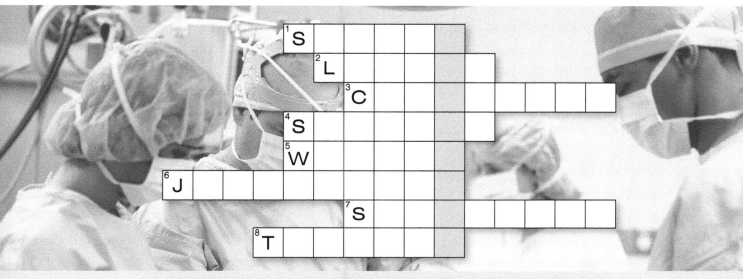

Complete the sentence with the word in the coloured squares.

Sally's brother wants to be a _____ on the six o'clock news.

Grammar Link

D Circle the correct words.

Following Your Heart

When John said that he wanted to become a fashion designer, his teacher said that he **(1)** may / should go to art school. His parents, however, told him that he **(2)** shouldn't / ought not become a fashion designer as he **(3)** ought to / might never become successful or make any money. They said he **(4)** ought to / may become a lawyer or a banker or that he **(5)** should / may think about studying medicine. His friends said that he **(6)** should / may not listen to his parents and that he **(7)** ought to / may study what he wanted, otherwise he **(8)** might / should regret it in the future. Thankfully, John agreed.

E Complete the second sentence so that it has a similar meaning to the first sentence. Use the correct form of should, ought to, may or might. More than one answer may be possible.

1 It's a good idea to start thinking about your future plans.
You _____ .

2 It's possible that Paul will get the job.
Paul _____ .

3 I wouldn't recommend choosing a career you don't like.
You _____ .

4 It's always possible that you won't achieve your ambition, but you must try.
You _____ .

5 I advise you to study harder if you want to get good grades.
You _____ .

6 There's a chance she'll achieve her goal if she tries hard enough.
She _____ .

7 It's wrong to be jealous of other people's success.
You _____ .

8 There's a possibility that he'll become a brilliant dancer.
He _____ .

F Match the beginnings of the sentences to their endings.

Beginnings	Endings
1 He wants to become a good athlete;	a you might get in next year.
2 He has injured his leg so	b she might not get into ballet school.
3 Although she's an excellent dancer,	c she should try to get into ballet school.
4 She's an excellent dancer and	d he ought to train hard every day.
5 It doesn't matter that you can't paint;	e you should still apply for the course.
6 He doesn't really like acting;	f he ought to change career.
7 The boy who played the leading role was very good;	g he might become a really famous actor one day.
8 Don't worry that you weren't accepted into art school,	h he might not be able to play in next week's game.

G In each sentence there is a word that is not needed. Circle the extra word.

1 You should study harder if you might want to become a doctor.

2 Sarah might not win the singing competition and become a big star.

3 If you might want to be the best, you should try your hardest!

4 You should not visit the Careers Advisory Service; they know which career is right for you.

5 People shouldn't be too ambitious; it may sometimes leads to disappointment.

6 There should to be equal opportunities so that men and women can both achieve their ambitions.

7 You should apply for the job; they will decide if you may have enough experience or not.

8 You shouldn't tell your boss you're leaving until you might find a new job.

Vocabulary Link

A Complete the paragraph with these words.

| brand | caught | curse | haunted | lake | luck | saucers | seriously | strangest | terribly |

A Bad Week!

The week he spent at the ancient (1) _____ castle in Scotland was one of the (2) _____ Arthur had ever had. He had gone there hoping to see one of the flying (3) _____ that had been reported to be in the sky in that area, but instead he had seven days of very bad (4) _____ . On the first day, while he was walking towards the (5) _____ , he fell and hurt his arm. On the fifth day, his car (6) _____ fire, and on the sixth day his (7) _____ new gold watch was stolen from his room and then he became (8) _____ ill after eating some local eggs for lunch! All in all, Arthur had been (9) _____ unlucky. Obviously, nobody had told him about the (10) _____ of the castle!

B Complete the sentences with these phrases.

| a tour of |
| afraid of |
| believe in |
| in an instant |
| make fun of |
| on a voyage |
| opinion of |
| work on |

1 Don't _____ me; I really did see a UFO!

2 What is the professor's _____ the new theory about crop circles?

3 Johnny decided to go on _____ the haunted castle.

4 Do you _____ fairies?

5 When they heard the house was haunted, they left _____ .

6 The scientist didn't really want to _____ the secret and mysterious project.

7 Of course I'm not _____ ghosts!

8 They were _____ across the Atlantic Ocean when her husband mysteriously disappeared.

C Use the words in capitals at the end of each sentence to make words which fit in the spaces.

1 Exactly how large were the _____ you saw? *FOOT*

2 A group of _____ are working on the Pyramids. *ARCHAEOLOGY*

3 He's the managing _____ of a mystery holiday company. *DIRECT*

4 It was quite _____ when the mummy began to move! *EXPECT*

5 'I think I've just seen a ghost!' '_____ you're imagining things!' *SURE*

6 How many ships have _____ in the Bermuda Triangle? *APPEAR*

7 Nathan gave the detective a _____ of what he'd seen. *DESCRIBE*

8 The truth about things like the Yeti and the Loch Ness Monster remains _____, but investigations are continuing. *KNOW*

D Complete the crossword.

Across

3 huge triangular buildings in Egypt

5 very old

7 hurt

9 There might be one in Loch Ness.

Down

1 a very large sea

2 There are a lot of these on TV.

4 a big creature with big feet that lives in the Himalayas

6 a dead body in ancient Egypt

8 a large group of trees

Now rearrange the letters in the coloured squares to make a word to complete the sentence.

Millie reads _____ stories because she loves mysteries.

Grammar Link

E Circle the correct words.

1 I wish I knew / had known about the ghost before I bought the house.

2 I wish I knew / had known more about the Loch Ness Monster.

3 They wish they had / had had a camera with them when they saw the UFO.

4 He wishes he hadn't lied / didn't lie about seeing the Yeti.

5 Sam wishes he were / would be a detective.

6 He wishes he saw / had seen the ghost too.

7 He wishes his mother would let him go / had let him go on the tour of the haunted castle next week.

8 She wishes she would see / had seen the Pyramids when they were in Egypt.

F Complete the text with *must* or *can't*.

Is There Anyone Out There?

Some people believe that there (1) _____ be life on other planets, because the universe is so big. This idea became more popular after 1947, when there were reports that a spacecraft had crashed in New Mexico. A spokesperson for the US government said, 'The pieces of metal found in the area (2) _____ be from a weather balloon.' However, one farmer said, 'That (3) _____ be true, because the metal was different from metals found on this planet.' In the 1990s, people became interested in the event again. One newspaper article said, 'The metal (4) _____ be from a spacecraft which crashed, because it's so unusual.' Even today, people (5) _____ be sure of what actually happened there. In that part of New Mexico, people often report sightings of UFOs, but the majority of people probably believe that such things (6) _____ exist. On the other hand, people who have seen them say they (7) _____ exist. I'm sure these people (8) _____ want scientists to investigate the theory that there is life on other planets.

G In each line of this paragraph there is a word that is not needed. Circle the extra word.

The Mystery of Stonehenge

1 I wish I would had visited Stonehenge when I was in Britain.

2 It must not be an amazing place. Although we know that the stones

3 came from a great distance, archaeologists can't to be sure that

4 the wheel existed at the time so they can't be work out how people

5 moved the stones. Some people believe that it was a temple and it must had

6 stay a holy place. Others think that this can't not be true, and that it

7 was used mainly as a calendar. Erich von Daniken said that it must be been a

8 landing guide for alien spacecraft. I wish we had knew why it was built.

Unit 15 Volunteers

Vocabulary Link

A Complete the text with these words.

> achievement available charity donate free member
> project raise unbelievable volunteers

Why Don't You Become a Volunteer?

Are you interested in helping to (1) _____ money to help poor families in Africa? Have you got some (2) _____ time to give us every weekend? If so, read on!

We need more (3) _____ to work in our (4) _____ shops across London. At the moment we're trying to make money for our new (5) _____ : a children's hospital. If you'd like to become a (6) _____ of our staff, please pick up a form – they're (7) _____ from all our shops – fill it in and return it to us.

So far, we've managed to raise an (8) _____ £50,000 towards our hospital. It's a great (9) _____ and you could help us to make it even greater. Pick up a form NOW!

If you don't have enough free time, but you would still like to help, you can (10) _____ some money.

Please contact Liz James on (01904) 623866.

B Complete the sentences with the correct form of these verbs.

> come help join look participate put run show

1 Mum's not here. She's _____ out at the local hospital shop this afternoon.

2 The students _____ in a sponsored swim last week and raised over £2,000.

3 The volunteers _____ away all the chairs after the concert.

4 Ethel can _____ back on both good and bad times in her thirty years of voluntary work.

5 The organisers were surprised by how many volunteers _____ forward to help.

6 Mr Davis has been _____ off the medal he received for 25 years' service as a voluntary firefighter.

7 The teacher offered to organise the school party for charity and she encouraged us all to _____ in.

8 You'll never guess who I _____ into at the charity shop today!

C Complete the words.

1   This word means to help out.   a _ _ _ _ _ _

2   This is another word for very clever.   b _ _ _ _ _ _

3   This is something that you get for doing something well.   a _ _ _ _

4   This is smaller than a town.   v _ _ _ _ _ _

5   You take this if you are ill.   m _ _ _ _ _ _ _

6   This piece of paper proves that you have passed an exam.   c _ _ _ _ _ _ _ _ _ _

Grammar Link

D Complete the second sentence so that it has a similar meaning to the first sentence. Use the passive.

1   We need volunteers to help us save endangered species.
    Volunteers _____ .

2   Volunteer doctors have improved the lives of many people.
    The lives of many people _____ .

3   They stopped the volunteer programmes because there wasn't enough money.
    The volunteer programmes _____ .

4   Volunteers are going to run the new recycling project.
    The new recycling project _____ .

5   Local volunteers developed this project.
    This project _____ .

6   Volunteers at the Animal Welfare Organisation have raised £1 million.
    £1 million _____ .

7   We will use donations to start new volunteer projects.
    Donations _____ .

8   The Cat Protection Society asked me to be a volunteer.
    I was _____ .

E Match the beginnings of the sentences to their endings.

Beginnings	Endings
1 Are more voluntary nurses required	a to organise the sponsored walk.
2 All volunteer firefighters	b by voluntary counsellors in some colleges.
3 Volunteer gardeners are needed	c for the health centre?
4 Students are given advice	d are expected to be ready in an emergency.
5 None of the people who helped at	e to clean up the local park.
6 The charity shop is run	f by volunteer sales staff.
7 Have you ever been asked	g the charity concert were paid.
8 The volunteers were asked	h to do voluntary work?

F Complete the paragraph with the correct form of the verbs in brackets. Use the passive. More than one answer may be possible.

Charity Lunch

Food is wasted every day. Did you know that millions of people could live on the food that
(1) _____ (throw away) every day? A famine lunch (2) _____
(organise) by the well-known charity *First for Famine* to make people aware of this and raise money for
their charity. The lunch (3) _____ (hold) next Saturday, 24th July and the organisers
hope that it (4) _____ (attend) by more than 300 people. The guests
(5) _____ (serve) a bowl of rice and they (6) _____ (ask) not to eat
anything else on that day. After lunch, a speech (7) _____ (make) by Maria Sanchez,
the volunteer director of *First for Famine*, and then there will be an auction of things which
(8) _____ (donate) by celebrities. *First for Famine* promise that all money
raised (9) _____ (use) to help starving people all over the world. Tickets for the event
(10) _____ (sell) at most major supermarkets for £100 each.

G Write a sentence for each of the situations. Use the passive. More than one answer may be possible.

1 the house / build / volunteers

_____

_____

4 the children / teach / volunteers / for six months

_____

_____

2 a water system / construct / volunteers

_____

_____

5 volunteers / want / a local charity

_____

_____

3 villagers / give / healthcare lessons / a doctor / every week

_____

_____

6 money / collect / for charity / all day yesterday

_____

_____

Unit 16 How Are You?

Vocabulary Link

A Circle the correct words.

Reflexology

When Sarah's headaches were (**1**) diagnosed / discovered as migraines, she decided to try reflexology, and went to a qualified (**2**) therapist / patient . She was extremely (**3**) serious / satisfied with the (**4**) treatment / conditions she received. She told us that reflexologists (**5**) massage / heal the feet to treat the whole body. Sarah said that each part of the foot (**6**) examined / represented a (**7**) specific / severe part of the body. 'Our feet are like a map of our bodies,' she explained. 'Reflexology certainly made me (**8**) feel / suffer much better!'

B Circle the odd one out.

1 glasses	bandage	optician	iridology
2 stripe	line	throat	dot
3 straightaway	finally	now	immediately
4 bad	serious	normal	severe
5 hay fever	stomach problems	allergy	operation
6 surgery	clinic	doctor	hospital
7 shoulders	heart	lungs	portion
8 disease	illness	cure	problem

C Use the words in capitals at the end of each sentence to make words which fit in the spaces.

1 I've got to write three _____ before I complete my medical training. *ASSIGN*

2 Do you know what your blood _____ is? *PRESS*

3 A _____ nose can mean you've got an allergy. *RUN*

4 I think you should see a _____ about your problem. *SPECIAL*

5 The doctor writes a _____ for my grandmother's medicine every month. *PRESCRIBE*

6 Make sure you choose a _____ alternative therapist. *QUALIFY*

7 She needs to do more tests to get an accurate _____ . *DIAGNOSE*

8 What's the _____ between our eyes and our illnesses? *CONNECT*

D Complete the words.

1 The doctor listens to your heart with this. s _ _ _ _ _ _ _ | _ _ _ _

2 Sometimes the nurse uses this to give you medicine. s _ _ _ _ _ _ |

3 The nurse might put this under your arm to see if you are ill. t _ _ _ _ _ _ _ |

4 This is where you sit until you see the doctor. w _ _ _ _ _ | r _ _ _

5 You sometimes put this around an injury. b _ _ _ _ _ _ |

6 This is what you have if your head hurts. h _ _ _ _ _ _ | _

7 You should have eight hours of this every night. s _ _ _ _

8 You should eat five portions of these every day. v _ _ _ _ _ _ | _ _

Grammar Link

E Read the paragaph and change the statements in bold into reported speech. Begin with the words given.

T'ai Chi*

Elderly people need to exercise as much as younger people, but as people get older this becomes more difficult. **(1) One well-known doctor said: 'T'ai chi is one of the best forms of exercise for elderly people.'** One reason for this is that it improves balance, so the elderly have fewer falls. **(2) One lady, Sally, said: 'It has been important for my health.'** **(3)** She continued by saying: **'I have made many new friends too.'** **(4) One t'ai chi instructor said: 'It has become popular because it is an easy form of exercise.'** **(5)** He continued: **'T'ai chi helps elderly people to become more active in their daily lives.'** **(6)** People who believe in the benefits of t'ai chi have said: **'Our lives have changed for the better because of it.'**

*a Chinese form of exercise that trains the body and mind in balance and control

---

1 One well-known doctor said _____

_____

2 Sally said _____

_____

3 She also said _____

_____

4 One t'ai chi instructor said _____

_____

5 He also said _____

_____

6 People who believe in the benefits of t'ai chi have said _____

_____

F Circle the correct words.

1 She said that she can't / **couldn't** do the exercises properly.

2 He said that he **was** / is going on a diet because his doctor had told him to.

3 Three years ago she told me that she had stopped eating red meat last year / **the year before** .

4 Last Monday, they said that they were going to an aerobics class tomorrow / **the following day** .

5 John said that he **had had** / had a good time at the gym yesteray.

6 Our family doctor said that we must / **had to** take more exercise.

7 Peter said that he will / **would** take me to the dentist's the next day.

8 Mary said that she **had been going** / had gone to physiotherapy for the last three months.

G Report what was said in each of the situations.

1 Robert said that _____

4 Mary said that _____

2 Jane said that _____

5 Bill said that _____

3 The doctor said that _____

6 Helen said that _____

Reading Link

A   Read the article quickly and find out what kind of people believe in the work that Amnesty International does.

Amnesty International

Ⓐ There are many voluntary organisations around the world. They are usually called NGOs (non-governmental organisations). This means that they do not belong to any government and that they are independent of all political parties.

Ⓑ One of the most well-known NGOs is called Amnesty International. When last counted, this organisation had more than 2.2 million members and supporters around the world. Although these supporters come from all over the world, and have different beliefs, they all believe in the work of Amnesty International.

Ⓒ Amnesty International's aim is to fight for human rights around the world. It wants to see a world where everybody can enjoy the rights that were written in what is called The Universal Declaration of Human Rights. This contains a list of human rights that all people should be able to enjoy. One of them, for example, is that nobody can ever be made a slave. Another one is that people should never be punished because of who they are or what they believe in.

Ⓓ Unfortunately, if we watch the news, we will see that people are being treated badly in many parts of the world. But, if organisations like Amnesty International didn't exist, then it's possible that things would be worse. When hundreds, or sometimes thousands, of people come together to show that they disagree with the way some people in the world are being treated, it is possible that the government or person who is treating them badly will listen and stop doing it.

Ⓔ Every person who joins Amnesty International helps to make its voice even louder. The next time you watch the news and see that something is happening in the world that you think is unfair, remember that you can add your voice to the 2.2 million voices of Amnesty International. Then you might be heard.

amnesty international
WORKING TO PROTECT HUMAN RIGHTS WORLDWIDE

B   Read the article again and answer the questions. Choose from paragraphs A-E.

Which paragraph(s)

gives examples of basic human rights?	**1** ☐
describes what an NGO is?	**2** ☐
mentions how many people belong to Amnesty International?	**3** ☐ **4** ☐
describes what Amnesty International tries to do?	**5** ☐
tells you what you can do?	**6** ☐
describes things not being perfect?	**7** ☐
mentions that the government can be forced to listen?	**8** ☐

Vocabulary Link

C Complete the table with these words and phrases.

> achievement   calories   charity   come forward   curse   determined   diagnose
> disappear   donate   excellent marks   goal   operation   raise money   sponsored walk
> strange   successful   surgeon   syringe   trick photography   unknown

Units 13-16

Ambitions	Mysteries	Volunteers	Health
_____	_____	_____	_____
_____	_____	_____	_____
_____	_____	_____	_____
_____	_____	_____	_____
_____	_____	_____	_____
_____	_____	_____	_____
_____	_____	_____	_____

Add any other appropriate words you learnt in Units 13-16 to the table.

Grammar Link

D Read the paragraph. For questions 1-8, choose the correct answer, a, b, or c.

A Visit to the Doctor

Mr Jones visited his doctor yesterday. He looked very worried, so the doctor told him to sit down and he asked him what was wrong. Mr Jones said, 'I think I'm dying. I wish I **(1)** _____ to see you much earlier.' The doctor thought that Mr Jones looked very healthy. 'He **(2)** _____ seriously ill,' he said to himself. He told Mr Jones that he **(3)** _____ panic and that he was sure that a solution to his problem could **(4)** _____ . Mr Jones said that every time he **(5)** _____ tea or coffee, he got a terrible pain in one of his eyes. Of course, the doctor wanted to know which eye hurt, but Mr Jones said that it **(6)** _____ always the same one. The doctor smiled and said that he knew what the problem **(7)** _____ . He told Mr Jones that the next time he drank tea or coffee, he **(8)** _____ take the teaspoon out of the cup first!

1	a	had come	b	came	c	would come
2	a	can't be	b	must be	c	should be
3	a	must	b	ought not to	c	can't
4	a	find	b	was found	c	be found
5	a	drank	b	drinks	c	was drinking
6	a	can't be	b	must be	c	wasn't
7	a	was	b	is	c	is being
8	a	can't have	b	can't	c	should

Unit 17 Fame

Vocabulary Link

A Complete the puzzle.

1 The film star _____ the reporters for his decision to leave the country.
2 I'd love to be a _____ and have my photograph taken all the time.
3 Do superstars feel _____ when they see silly pictures of themselves in the newspaper?
4 The tickets for the concert were sold out _____ minutes.
5 Hundreds of _____ were all pointing their cameras at the same person.
6 You might think he's telling the truth about being famous, but I smell a _____ !
7 The young reporter is very excited because she's going to _____ Brad Pitt tomorrow!
8 Is it true that Hood's latest film broke all box _____ records?
9 He says the worst thing about being _____ is that he doesn't have a private life.
10 I don't know his face, but his name _____ a bell.

Complete the sentence with the word in the coloured squares.

Who is the _____ star in sunglasses and a big hat?

B Underline the wrong word in each of the sentences and write the correct word.

1 Jake likes to hang on with his friends at clubs to see celebrities. _____
2 The band is in the studio releasing an album at the moment. _____
3 Tickets for the rock concert sold off within a few days. _____
4 They really put a winner with this rock group. _____
5 'I don't like discussing my private life on talking shows,' said the singer. _____
6 His latest film has done a killing at box offices around the world. _____

C Complete the text with these words.

attention	autograph	ceremony	fans	jetted
manager	posed	reporters	shaking	superstar

Famous Actress Comes to Town

Heathrow Airport was busier than usual last night as hundreds of (1) _____ gathered, hoping to see their favourite (2) _____ , Dolores Fostrup, or even get her (3) _____ .

Dolores, who has (4) _____ halfway around the world in the last two weeks, caught the (5) _____ of the world's film-lovers when she received not one, but two awards at the recent Golden Planet Award (6) _____ in Hollywood.

As Ms Fostrup made her way through the airport, everyone, including many film magazine photographers and (7) _____ who were there, rushed forward. Surrounded by several airport security staff and her (8) _____ , Dolores spent a short time (9) _____ hands with as many people as she could. She also (10) _____ for a few photographs before being driven off to the comfort of her luxury hotel suite in central London.

Grammar Link

D Match the beginnings of the sentences to their endings.

Beginnings	Endings
1 At the concert, the boy asked Madonna	**a** he had chosen to film in the jungle.
2 The chat show host asked the actress	**b** whether she would give him her autograph.
3 They asked the director why	**c** where he had hurt himself.
4 The journalist asked the band	**d** she enjoyed being on TV.
5 They asked the director	**e** if he had chosen to film in the desert.
6 She asked the injured football player	**f** if they had always wanted to be famous.
7 The reporter asked the weather girl if	**g** why they were retiring.
8 They asked the reality show contestants	**h** how long she had been a waitress before getting a role.

E Circle the correct words.

1   He asked the famous writer if he could / can sign the book for him.

2   The policeman asked the girls if they are / were waiting for the actor.

3   The fans asked the tennis player if she thought / thinks she would win the tournament.

4   The pop star asked if the reporters will / would leave him alone.

5   They asked her if she had ever / ever met the politician.

6   He asked her if she had realised / realised she would become so famous.

7   They asked the photographer how long he had / had he been taking photographs of models.

8   The photographer asked the actress if she wants / wanted to pose for some photographs.

F Complete the second sentence so that it has a similar meaning to the first. Use reported speech.

1 'How did you get the role in your latest film?' asked the interviewer.
The interviewer asked the actor _____.

2 'When is your new CD coming out?' asked the TV presenter.
The TV presenter asked the rock band _____.

3 'Mum, can I go to the rock concert?' asked Sally.
Sally asked her mum _____.

4 'Have you seen your favourite footballer's new haircut, David?' asked his sister.
His sister asked David _____.

5 'Are you going to ask for Leonardo DiCaprio's autograph, Janice?' asked Peter.
Peter asked Janice _____.

6 'Did you really have your photograph taken with Johnny Depp?'
She asked him _____.

7 'Were there many other reporters waiting outside the hotel?' the editor asked.
The editor asked the reporter _____.

8 'Which member of the band writes the songs?' asked the reporter.
The reporter asked the singer _____.

G Read the paragraph and change the sentences in bold into reported speech. Begin with the words given.

Bad Communication

The interview with the film star had been the most difficult one the reporter had ever had to do. The actor had hardly spoken. **(1) Firstly, she asked him, 'Did you dream of becoming an actor when you were a child?'** He replied, 'What a silly question!' **(2) Then she asked him, 'Are you enjoying your time in Rome?'** **(3) 'Are you planning to stay for a long time?'** she continued. He just answered 'Yes.' She then tried asking him about his latest film. **(4) She asked him, 'Did you enjoy filming in India?'** **(5) 'What did you think of the country?'** she continued. He said, 'It was nice,' and then smiled. She was beginning to get angry. **(6) She went on to ask him, 'Do you have any plans for a new film?'** 'Yes, I do,' he said. **(7) She quickly asked him, 'Can you tell me about them?'** 'No', he replied, 'it's too soon.' She couldn't control herself anymore. **(8) She asked him, 'Why did you agree to do an interview if you don't like doing them?'** 'Oh, I like interviews,' he said, 'I'm just not sure I like you!'

1 Firstly, she asked him _____.

2 Then she asked him _____.

3 She went on to ask him _____.

4 She asked him _____.

5 She went on to ask him _____.

6 She went on to ask him _____.

7 She quickly asked him _____.

8 She asked him _____.

Unit 18 Celebrate!

Vocabulary Link

A Circle the correct words.

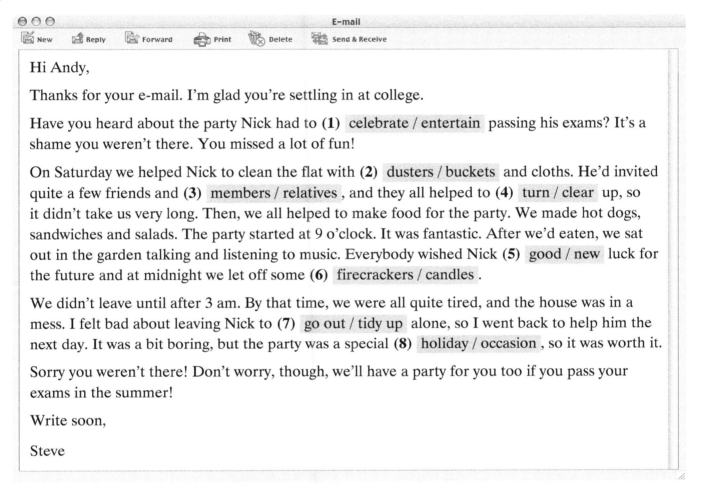

E-mail

New   Reply   Forward   Print   Delete   Send & Receive

Hi Andy,

Thanks for your e-mail. I'm glad you're settling in at college.

Have you heard about the party Nick had to **(1)** celebrate / entertain passing his exams? It's a shame you weren't there. You missed a lot of fun!

On Saturday we helped Nick to clean the flat with **(2)** dusters / buckets and cloths. He'd invited quite a few friends and **(3)** members / relatives , and they all helped to **(4)** turn / clear up, so it didn't take us very long. Then, we all helped to make food for the party. We made hot dogs, sandwiches and salads. The party started at 9 o'clock. It was fantastic. After we'd eaten, we sat out in the garden talking and listening to music. Everybody wished Nick **(5)** good / new luck for the future and at midnight we let off some **(6)** firecrackers / candles .

We didn't leave until after 3 am. By that time, we were all quite tired, and the house was in a mess. I felt bad about leaving Nick to **(7)** go out / tidy up alone, so I went back to help him the next day. It was a bit boring, but the party was a special **(8)** holiday / occasion , so it was worth it.

Sorry you weren't there! Don't worry, though, we'll have a party for you too if you pass your exams in the summer!

Write soon,

Steve

B Complete the sentences with these phrasal verbs.

dress up	get together	give out	go round	let off	put away	put on	take out

1 Don't forget to _____ all the glasses after the party.

2 Sandy says we have to _____ for her party on Saturday.

3 Let's _____ next weekend and go to the fireworks display.

4 I know it's a fancy-dress party, but I'm not going to _____ these clothes!

5 It's traditional to _____ fireworks on New Year's Eve in some countries.

6 It's my sister's birthday, so I think I'll _____ to her house tonight; do you want to come?

7 Who does Chris want to _____ on his 21st birthday?

8 Have you had time to _____ the invitations?

C Underline the wrong word in each of the sentences below and write the correct word.

1 It's my parents' 25th wedding celebration tomorrow. _____

2 Have you been invited to Alice's fancy-clothes party? _____

3 We passed a great time at the disco! _____

4 I hope Mike remembers to close the hall for the graduation party. _____

5 Rosie took first prize for best dancer at the end-of-term party. _____

6 Simon went out to celebrate when he passed his driving exam. _____

D Use the words in capitals at the end of each sentence to make words which fit in the spaces.

1 We _____ need more CDs for the party.   *DEFINITE*

2 I'm not sure if those jeans are really _____ for an anniversary party!   *SUIT*

3 That was the most _____ party I've been to for ages.   *ENJOY*

4 She prepared a _____ dinner to celebrate her birthday.   *WONDER*

5 The Chinese New Year changes according to the _____ of the moon.   *MOVE*

6 We thought a clown would _____ up the party and make it more lively.   *BRIGHT*

7 After the _____ ceremony, we went for a Chinese meal to celebrate.   *GRADUATE*

8 Alice made the _____ room look just like a real disco for the party.   *LIVE*

Grammar Link

E Circle the correct words.

1 I think that is the tastier / tastiest birthday cake I have ever had.

2 This year's fireworks were louder / more loud than last year's; they hurt my ears!

3 The carnival in Rio de Janeiro gets bigger / more big every year.

4 The party went on much longer / longest than expected.

5 New Year is more / most popular in Scotland than it is in England.

6 Philip thought the party was worst / the worst he had ever been to.

7 The graduation ball is going to take place in the most / more expensive hotel in the area.

8 Some of the richer / richest people in the world were at the party.

F Decide which phrase, a or b, completes the second sentence in each pair, so that both sentences have a similar meaning.

1 The third day of the festival is more popular than the other two.
The third day is _____ day of the festival.
  a most popular   **b** the most popular

2 The decorations this year were not as colourful as last year's.
Last year's decorations were _____ this year's.
  a more colourful than   **b** the more colourful

3 She had never danced so much at a party.
She danced _____ she had ever danced at a party.
  a more than   **b** the most than

4 This year, there was more food and drink at the party than last year.
Last year, there was _____ at the party than this year.
  a less food and drink   **b** least food and drink

5 Harry's costume was more brightly-coloured than all the others at the ball.
Harry's costume was _____ at the ball.
  a the most brightly-coloured   **b** the more brightly-coloured

6 Last year's Chinese New Year was earlier than this year's.
This year's Chinese New Year was _____ last year's.
  a earlier than   **b** later than

7 I have never been to such an interesting festival!
This is _____ festival I have ever been to!
  a the least interesting   **b** the most interesting

8 No other carnival in the world is as big as the carnival in Rio De Janeiro.
The carnival in Rio De Janeiro is _____ the world.
  a the biggest in   **b** bigger than

G Complete the sentences with the correct form of the words in brackets. Use the comparative and the superlative.

Notting Hill Carnival

The Notting Hill Carnival in London started as a small street party in 1964. At the time, the Caribbean immigrants who had moved to London were facing difficulties such as racism and poor job opportunities, so they decided to organise a festival to make everyone in the area **(1)** _____ (happy) and to create an even **(2)** _____ (strong) sense of community. The festival used to be much **(3)** _____ (small) then than it is today. Every year, the carnival gets **(4)** _____ (big) and some people say that it is the **(5)** _____ (large) street party in Europe. Nowadays, the carnival has become **(6)** _____ (popular) than ever before and over a period of three days, approximately 3 million people dance in the streets of Notting Hill. It is, for many Caribbean immigrants living in London, one of their **(7)** _____ (proud) achievements. Personally, I think that the **(8)** _____ (good) thing about it is that anyone can take part!

Unit 19 Advertising

Vocabulary Link

A Circle the correct words.

My Working Day

Here at *Glad-Ads Advertising Agency*, no two days are the same.
That's what makes our job so **(1)** impressive / challenging .

Every day is **(2)** filled / reminded with all kinds of different
jobs. I spend a few hours in the morning
(3) presenting / thinking of slogans for a chocolate
(4) company / client , and then after lunch I might be trying to
find a new **(5)** offer / jingle for sports shoes. I also work with our
designers on **(6)** media / logos for new clients. The company spends a lot of time doing
(7) advert / market research so that we can see what other advertisers are doing. For the same
reason, we look at the designs for different **(8)** billboards / screens by other companies, and we
look through hundreds of magazines every month just to see the advertisements.

It's always really exciting when we've got the final **(9)** noticeboard / version of an advertisement
ready for a new campaign. And the first time we see our new advertisement during a commercial
(10) agency / break or in a magazine is fabulous – that's what makes all the hard work worth it.

B Complete the sentences with the correct form of these verbs and phrases.

| come up with |
| depend on |
| free of |
| hear about |
| interested in |
| send to |
| spend on |
| take over |

1 I _____ that new advertisement from a friend.

2 You can advertise in our local newspaper _____ charge.

3 Jenny's not _____ watching commercials. She always changes channel when they come on.

4 Companies _____ a lot of money _____ publicity.

5 Carl's _____ a letter _____ the managing director of the company, complaining about their billboards.

6 You can always _____ *Snackabite* to find imaginative slogans for their products.

7 What new logo have they _____ for strawberry cola?

8 When an advertisement has been filmed, the editing team _____ .

C Complete the puzzle.

1 Advertisers want as much _____ for their products as possible.
2 Julian's trying to think up the words for the _____ to go with the new product.
3 In my opinion, too many _____ are full of adverts.
4 With the _____ _____ , I can change channels quickly when the commercials come on TV.
5 One day, adverts could be sent to the moon using _____ .
6 They decided to use cartoon _____ in their adverts.
7 Maybe it wasn't such a good idea to stick an advert to the side of a space _____ .
8 They need to _____ products attractively in shops.
9 I think it's _____ incredible that companies want to advertise on the moon!
10 When are they going to _____ that new Russian rocket into space?

Complete the sentence with the word in the coloured squares.

It must have been quite difficult, filming a _____ aboard a space station.

Grammar Link

D Match the beginnings of the sentences to their endings.

Beginnings		Endings	
1	This is the commercial	a	which were spoiling the city's skyline.
2	Thankfully, they have taken down the huge billboards	b	whose friends tell them they should buy what's being advertised.
3	My aunt is the kind of person	c	which was shown all over the world.
4	We were very pleased	d	who buys anything advertised on TV.
5	That's the owner of the company	e	when they want to promote a new product.
6	It's very annoying for people	f	where my old school used to be.
7	Offices for an advertising company are being built	g	whose latest product is being advertised at every bus stop.
8	Companies sometimes spend thousands of pounds	h	when the TV channel stopped showing the shocking advertisement.

E Circle the correct words.

1 This is the commercial who / which cost £2 million to make.
2 The jingle which / when you hear on the pizza advert was written by a famous musician.
3 There isn't a football player which / who doesn't have a company logo on their sports kit.
4 The old lady which / who lives next door believes everything they say in advertisements.
5 The advert whose / where slogan was 'It's for you-hoo!' was for a British telephone company.
6 Between 9 and 11 o'clock in the morning is when / where there are no adverts on the radio.
7 The park is the only place which / where there are no billboards!
8 Surely, there can't be anyone whose / who isn't influenced by adverts in some way!

F In each sentence there is a word that is not needed. Circle the extra word.

1 There are many people who believe everything whose adverts say.
2 We have complained to the company whose billboard blocks our view to where the sea.
3 I only watch movies when on TV channels which don't have commercials.
4 She who likes special offers for new products.
5 Sometimes there are jingles which are so successful when everybody remembers them.
6 Adverts for children's toys which are shown when most children are watching television.
7 TV channels which make money only through advertising whose are really boring.
8 The organisation whose job it is to make sure which adverts don't lie, sometimes takes companies to court.

G Complete the paragraph with when, where, which, who or whose.

Selling Truth or Lies?

It can sometimes be very upsetting for parents (1) _____ children ask for very expensive toys and clothes (2) _____ have been advertised on TV. It isn't surprising that children want the things (3) _____ they see in adverbs. Adverts have become part of our everyday lives and they are everywhere. There isn't a time of day (4) _____ we are not confronted with advertisements. On the television or radio, at bus stops, on billboards in the streets, there isn't a single place (5) _____ there is no advertising. Although the purpose of advertising is to sell products, there are many people (6) _____ lives are affected negatively by it. It's not just difficult for parents (7) _____ are asked by their children for expensive items, but also for many people (8) _____ are disappointed because a product is not as good as the advertisement said it would be.

Unit 20 Phobias

Vocabulary Link

A Complete the paragraph with these words.

> behaviour   complicated   condition   controlled   encouraged   face   fear   suffered

Not Afraid Any More

Joe had **(1)** _____ from a **(2)** _____ of meeting new people ever since he was a child. This **(3)** _____ had always made his life extremely **(4)** _____ . When he heard about **(5)** _____ therapy on a TV documentary, he decided to go and see a therapist. By that time, Joe didn't really want to come in contact with anybody he didn't know. He was even beginning to find going to work a problem. The therapist **(6)** _____ Joe to confront his problem, so he started thinking about meeting new people, and then, after a few weeks, he started meeting them in a **(7)** _____ way. It wasn't all that long before Joe learned to **(8)** _____ his fears and now he's even managed to start going to parties on his own!

B Circle the correct words.

1   I didn't think she would ever get / go over her fear of heights.

2   How do you face / cope with your mother's phobia of cats?

3   She decided to hold / keep her fears to herself.

4   I know / hear of a man who is afraid of water.

5   I was upset, so my son got / took up the story and finished it for me.

6   You can't lead / affect a normal life if you are too scared to go out.

C Complete the words.

1 This is somebody's opinion about what someone else should do. a _ _ _ _ _

2 You might feel this when you are very afraid. p _ _ _ _

3 These are tiny creatures with six legs. i _ _ _ _ _

4 This is another word for an operation. s _ _ _ _ _ _

5 This is what we call a large group of people. c _ _ _ _

6 These are tiny things we can't see but which can make us ill. g _ _ _ _

7 This word means to stop something from happening. p _ _ _ _ _ _

8 This person might make you go to sleep! h _ _ _ _ _ _ _ _

D Use the words in capitals at the end of each sentence to make words which fit in the spaces.

1 It took Elsa three months to recover from her _____ . *OPERATE*

2 Terry's trying to control the _____ he has whenever he sees a frog. *REACT*

3 Lynn hopes the _____ will be able to help her. *PSYCHOLOGY*

4 Joe's fear of _____ makes life very difficult for him. *HIGH*

5 After only four _____ with the therapist, Lara was able to face her worst fears. *MEET*

6 Susie was _____ when the spider landed on her head! *TERROR*

7 Paul still finds it _____ to be in open spaces, but he's better than he was. *STRESS*

8 Many people have got a phobia of _____ snakes! *POISON*

Grammar Link

E Circle the correct words.

1 Sally avoids to get / getting on buses because she hates being in crowded places.

2 John didn't want to go / going up the Eiffel Tower because he's afraid of heights.

3 She failed warning / to warn her mother that her pet snake had escaped from her bedroom.

4 The doctor asked the patient if she minded having / to have therapy for her fear of flying.

5 She managed jumping / to jump up onto the kitchen table when she saw the mouse!

6 She refused to move / moving her dog even though she knew the little boy was frightened.

7 He admits to scream / screaming when he saw the spider, but not that he fainted.

8 The naughty boy considered to put / putting his little sister in the lift because he knew she was terrified of them.

F Decide which phrase, a or b, completes the second sentence in each pair, so that both sentences have a similar meaning.

1 I won't invite her to the bungee jump because she won't come.
   It's no use _____ her to the bungee jump because she won't come.
   a inviting   **b** to invite

2 She'll never attempt a parachute jump. She's scared of heights!
   She'll never risk _____ a parachute jump. She's scared of heights!
   a to do   **b** doing

3 I won't fly in a plane!
   I refuse _____ in a plane.
   a flying   **b** to fly

4 He's scared of people, can you imagine that?
   Can you imagine _____ scared of people?
   a being   **b** to be

5 Tom is slowly getting over his phobia.
   Tom is learning _____ with his phobia.
   a coping   **b** to cope

6 If you see a therapist, you might stop being scared of insects.
   You might stop being scared of insects by _____ a therapist.
   a seeing   **b** to see

7 It's a waste of time asking him to go swimming; he's scared of water.
   There's no point _____ him to go swimming; he's scared of water.
   a to ask   **b** asking

8 'OK, Mum, I'll get in the lift with you if you hold my hand,' he said.
   He agreed _____ in the lift with his mother if she held his hand.
   a getting   **b** to get

G Complete the paragraph with the correct form of the verbs in brackets. More than one answer may be possible.

Fight or Flight

Many people have attempted **(1)** _____ (deal) with their phobias, and some even decide **(2)** _____ (visit) a doctor or therapist. One type of therapy promises **(3)** _____ (be) the most effective. When in danger, all creatures seem **(4)** _____ (react) in the same way. The heart beats much faster and the blood rushes through the body. This is called the 'fight or flight' reaction, which means that the body plans **(5)** _____ (fight) for its life or run as fast as it can; in other words, 'take flight'. However, the body can't keep **(6)** _____ (do) this for long; after a while, it must slow down again. Therapists have discovered that by **(7)** _____ (lock) people in an empty room with what they are scared of, they will feel all the symptoms of the 'fight or flight' reaction. Their hearts will beat fast and they may even start **(8)** _____ (scream), but at some point, the body will have to slow down again. They will then find themselves in a calm state. The brain records this information and the next time they see the thing they are afraid of, they will remember to stay calm.

Reading Link

A Read the article quickly and find out why people might want to get out of the TV show.

I'm a Celebrity, Get Me Out of Here!

Every year in Britain a number of famous people get the opportunity to appear in the country's most popular reality TV show, *I'm a Celebrity, Get Me Out of Here!* And, even though the conditions on the show are absolutely awful and the contestants all have to complete some very nasty challenges, the celebrities who are asked to take part are almost always happy to do so. One celebrity said recently, on leaving the jungle, that it was the most enjoyable thing he had ever done in his life!

The show takes place in the specially-adapted surroundings of part of the Australian countryside. Temperatures there during filming reach over 36 degrees Celsius. The celebrities live in very basic shelters, taking their drinking water from the nearby stream and using the billabongs (natural pools) to provide both bathing and laundry facilities. Swimming, if done at all, is done in the billabongs too. The area is home to the world's most dangerous animals, so the celebrities have to avoid these to survive.

The show attracts huge audiences every night, and viewers vote weekly to say who they think should leave the jungle that week. While they are there, the contestants have to try to complete various challenges, many of them involving overcoming their worst personal fears and phobias. Regular challenges include things like eating insects or worms, or being buried alive in a glass coffin with live rats crawling all over them! Sometimes the celebrities manage to surprise themselves when they discover they're able to do things they'd never dreamt they could. 'Eating the worms was unbelievably awful,' said one celebrity who was voted out of the jungle in the first two weeks of the show. She admitted that she had had bad dreams about it for days afterwards.

One reason the show is so popular is that viewers get the chance to see the rich and famous in completely different situations. By the end of the show, when the new king or queen of the jungle has been voted for by over three million viewers, the few remaining contestants are dirty, angry and have often argued and fought with each other. They certainly don't look anything like rich and famous celebrities!

B Read the article again. For questions 1-6, choose the correct answer, a, b or c.

1 How do most celebrities feel when they are asked to go on the show?
  a They are worried about the nasty challenges.
  b They want to go on the show.
  c They think it will be absolutely awful.

2 What are the billabongs used for?
  a for washing and swimming
  b only for swimming
  c to provide drinking water

3 How can viewers affect the show?
  a They are involved in the challenges.
  b They can vote for the celebrities.
  c They decide which celebrities take part in the show.

4 What surprises some of the celebrities when they are in the jungle?
  a They have bad dreams after the show.
  b They manage to complete the challenges.
  c The challenges are so awful.

5 What makes the show so popular?
  a Viewers like to see famous people arguing.
  b Every contestant is different.
  c Viewers don't usually see celebrities looking like this.

6 What is true about the king or queen of the jungle by the end of the show?
  a They are often dirty and angry.
  b They have fought with the other celebrities.
  c They have received over three million votes.

Vocabulary Link

C Complete the table with these words and phrases.

> anniversary   autograph   billboard   cure   dress up   entertainment
> fan   fear   hypnotist   invitation   jingle   logo   market research   panic
> performance   pop star   private life   reporter   slogan   terror

Units 17-20

Fame	Celebrations	Advertising	Phobias

Add any other appropriate words you learnt in Units 17-20 to the table.

Grammar Link

D Read the paragraph. For questions 1-8, choose the correct answer, a, b, or c.

Forever Famous

Imagine **(1)** _____ so famous that absolutely everybody in the world knows your name and recognises your face immediately. One such person was Marilyn Monroe. Although she has now been dead for **(2)** _____ than she was alive, her name is still known by people of all nationalities and ages. Some have said that she is probably the **(3)** _____ famous woman of the 20th century. She was born in 1926 and she spent most of her childhood in foster homes and orphanages as her mother, **(4)** _____ had psychological problems, was permanently in hospital. This is probably why, many years later, when she was asked if she **(5)** _____ she would become famous, she answered, 'I knew I belonged to the public and the world, not because I was talented or even beautiful, but because I had never belonged to anything or anyone else.' She was discovered at an early age by a photographer and she quickly became a very successful model, but she wanted **(6)** _____ an actress. Soon after that, she managed **(7)** _____ roles in films and in 1953, she was voted 'Best New Actress' by a magazine called *Photoplay*. By the time she died mysteriously in 1962, she had made 30 films. She is still considered **(8)** _____ just as modern an image as she was fifty years ago.

1	a	to be	b	being	c	have been
2	a	long	b	longer	c	longest
3	a	more	b	most	c	much
4	a	which	b	where	c	who
5	a	did know	b	knows	c	had known
6	a	to become	b	becoming	c	became
7	a	getting	b	to get	c	got
8	a	being	b	is	c	to be

Extra Practice   Units 1-4

Complete the crossword.

Across

3   a programme of study

6   another word for gifted

7   a story from ancient or past times that may be true or not

11 a work of art that is made out of stone or wood

13 a computer screen

14 a person whose job it is to save people in danger in the sea

15 the ability to remember things

Down

1   the thing you put your canvas on to paint

2   collect

4   serious and dangerous situation which needs immediate action

5   a university teacher

8   a picture made using a pencil

9   sure that you want to do something

10 simple medical help given before a doctor arrives

12 ability to be brave and do something dangerous

Now rearrange the letters in the coloured squares to make a word to complete the sentence.

The local _____ are responsible for keeping beaches safe and clean.

Complete the puzzle.

1 _____ are much smaller than ordinary computers.

2 There are hundreds of endangered animals which are facing _____ .

3 The best way to see an island is to go on a boat _____ .

4 The telephone is one method of _____ .

5 Some organisations send _____ to their members regularly.

6 If you don't eat, you will _____ .

7 Mobile phones don't work without _____ .

8 A very rich person is a _____ .

9 An _____ works for someone else.

10 An _____ is a person who teaches a sport.

Complete the sentence with the word in the coloured squares.

The _____ of Britain is about 61 million.

Complete the crossword.

Across

2 stay alive

4 money used in a particular country

6 another word for boring

7 another word for notice

8 the ability to wait without getting angry

9 ask firmly for something

12 things that are for sale

13 take in air

15 another word for specialist

Down

1 another word for proof

3 you use these to help you walk when you've got a broken leg

5 costing a lot of money

10 the total quantity of something

11 exchange goods or services for other goods or services

14 being ready to act

Now rearrange the letters in the coloured squares to make a word to complete the sentence.

How much _____ do you need to become a nurse?

A   Find fifteen words.

```
X T D V O Y A G E D F S
H H O S M W A I T E R T
C E C S M A P Z M S P E
Y R U T M S Y B U E T T
C M M A E U R S S R G H
O O E F D R A E I T E O
L M N F I G M C C E O S
A E T S C E I R I R N C
K T A Y I O D G A M D O
E E R P N N X D N A R P
P R Y D E T E C T I V E
G S E C R E T A R Y U I
```

B   Complete the sentences with the words from task A.

1   She plays the violin very well, but she doesn't want to be a _____ when she grows up.

2   Jake's working as a _____ in a café to help pay for his studies.

3   Jane wants to become a _____ but she needs to improve her typing and computer skills.

4   Is the Sahara the largest _____ in the world?

5   A doctor uses a _____ to listen to a patient's heartbeat.

6   My mum took my temperature with a _____ .

7   We lost the _____ on the sponsored walk and had to ask a local farmer the way.

8   Has the doctor prescribed any _____ for your stomach problems?

9   The archaeologist wants to work in a _____ and find an ancient Egyptian mummy!

10   Hercule Poirot is a famous _____ in Agatha Christie's crime novels.

11   They say that the Loch Ness monster lives in a _____ in Scotland.

12   The _____ did the operation last week, and I'm feeling fine now.

13   The _____ across the Atlantic Ocean on the cruise ship was amazing.

14   All the teaching _____ at our school helped organise the trip to Egypt.

15   I watched a very interesting _____ about the curse of the mummy.

Complete the crossword.

Across

1   stop something from happening

3   another word for ashamed

4   a journey into space

9   another word for surgery

10 a family member who lived a long time ago

12 say that somebody is responsible for something

13 another word for recommend

14 grass that grows in the sea

Down

1   attention given to somebody or something by TV and newspapers

2   being very afraid

5   another word for strange

6   a cloth you use to clean around the house with

7   a family member

8   another word for puzzled

11 say no

Now rearrange the letters in the coloured squares to make a word to complete the sentence.

How shall we _____ the house for New Year's Eve?